Applied Data Visu R and ggplot2

Create useful, elaborate, and visually appealing plots

Dr. Tania Moulik

BIRMINGHAM - MUMBAI

Applied Data Visualization with R and ggplot2

Acquisitions Editor: Aditya Date
Content Development Editors: Darren Patel, Tanmayee Patil
Production Coordinator: Arvindkumar Gupta

First published: September 2018

Production reference: 1270918

Published by Packt Publishing Ltd.
Livery Place
35 Livery Street
Birmingham
B3 2PB, UK.

ISBN 978-1-78961-215-8

www.packtpub.com

About the Author

Dr. Tania Moulik has a PhD in particle physics. She worked at CERN and the Tevatron at Fermi National Accelerator Laboratory in IL, USA. She has worked with C++, Python, and R. She also worked in big data projects and grid computing. She has a passion for data analysis and likes to share her knowledge with others who would like to delve into the world of data analytics. She especially likes R and ggplot2 as a powerful analytics package.

`mapt.io`

Mapt is an online digital library that gives you full access to over 5,000 books and videos, as well as industry leading tools to help you plan your personal development and advance your career. For more information, please visit our website.

Why Subscribe?

- Spend less time learning and more time coding with practical eBooks and Videos from over 4,000 industry professionals

- Improve your learning with Skill Plans built especially for you

- Get a free eBook or video every month

- Mapt is fully searchable
- Copy and paste, print, and bookmark content

PacktPub.com

Did you know that Packt offers eBook versions of every book published, with PDF and ePub files available? You can upgrade to the eBook version at `www.PacktPub.com` and as a print book customer, you are entitled to a discount on the eBook copy. Get in touch with us at `service@packtpub.com` for more details.

At `www.PacktPub.com`, you can also read a collection of free technical articles, sign up for a range of free newsletters, and receive exclusive discounts and offers on Packt books and eBooks.

Table of Contents

Preface

This book introduces you to the world of data visualization by talking about the basic features of ggplot2. Learn all about setting up the R environment and then begin exploring features of ggplot2. Grammar of graphics and geometric objects are the fundamentals you must know before you dive deep into the plotting techniques. Read and discover what are layers, scales, coordinates, and themes, and explore how you can use them to transform your data into aesthetical graphs. Learn the simple plots, such as histograms, and then some advanced plots, such as superimposing plots and density plots. Learn to plot trends, correlations, and statistical summaries. After reading this book, your data visualizations will wow clients.

After completing this book, you will be able to:

- Set up the R environment, RStudio, and explain structure of ggplot2
- Distinguish types of variables and use best practices to visualize them
- Change visualization defaults to reveal more information about data
- Implement the grammar of graphics in ggplot2 such as scales and faceting
- Build complex, aesthetic visualizations with ggplot2 analysis methods
- Logically and systematically explore complex relationships
- Compare variables in a single visual, with advanced plotting methods

Who This Book Is For

This book is meant for professionals, who work with data and R, and for students, who want to enhance their data analysis skills by adding informative and professional visualizations. We assume that readers know basics of the R language, its commands, and objects.

What This Book Covers

Chapter 1, *Basic Plotting in ggplot2*, will help you to understand Kubernetes patterns which would be presented with the examples from Kubernetes itself and external applications.

Chapter 2, *Grammar of Graphics and Visual Components*, will help you to cover accessing Kubernetes API with raw HTTP queries to complex libraries with both in-cluster and out-cluster examples.

Chapter 3, *Advanced Geoms And Statistics*, will present extension capabilities of Kubernetes with custom resource definitions, custom controllers, dynamic admission controllers, and custom schedulers.

To Get the Most out of This Book

For an optimal experience, we recommend the following hardware configuration:

- Processor: Intel Core i5 or equivalent
- Memory: 4GB RAM
- Storage: 35 GB available space

You'll also need the following software installed in advance:

- OS: Windows 7 SP1 64-bit, Windows 8.1 64-bit, or Windows 10 64-bit
- Browser: Google Chrome, Latest Version
- **Installing R**:

1. To install the R package and libraries, go to http://cran.us.r-project.org/ in your browser.
2. Click on **Download R for Windows**, click on base, then click on **Download R 3.5.0 for Windows** (or any newer version that appears).
3. Install R. Leave all default settings as they are in the installation options.

- **Installing RStudio**:

1. To install RStudio, go to http://rstudio.org/download/desktop.
2. Choose the default installation.
3. Open RStudio after installation. It uses the underlying R package and will open it automatically in the IDE.

Download the Example Code Files

You can download the example code files for this book from your account at www.packtpub.com. If you purchased this book elsewhere, you can visit www.packtpub.com/support and register to have the files emailed directly to you.

You can download the code files by following these steps:

1. Log in or register at www.packtpub.com.
2. Select the **SUPPORT** tab.

3. Click on **Code Downloads & Errata**.
4. Enter the name of the book in the **Search** box and follow the onscreen instructions.

Once the file is downloaded, please make sure that you unzip or extract the folder using the latest version of:

- WinRAR/7-Zip for Windows
- Zipeg/iZip/UnRarX for Mac
- 7-Zip/PeaZip for Linux

The code bundle for the book is also hosted on GitHub at https://github.com/ TrainingByPackt/Applied-Data-Visualization-with-R-and-ggplot2. In case there's an update to the code, it will be updated on the existing GitHub repository.

We also have other code bundles from our rich catalog of books and videos available at https://github.com/PacktPublishing/. Check them out!

Conventions Used

There are a number of text conventions used throughout this book.

CodeInText: Indicates code words in text, database table names, folder names, filenames, file extensions, pathnames, dummy URLs, user input, and Twitter handles. Here is an example: "Use the ggplot(df_vanc,aes(x=Vancouver)) + geom_bar() command to obtain the following chart."

A block of code is set as follows:

```
df_t <- read.csv("data/historical-hourly-weather-data/temperature.csv")
ggplot(df_t,aes(x=Vancouver))+geom_histogram()
ggplot(df_t,aes(x=Miami))+geom_histogram();
```

Activity: These are scenario-based activities that will let you practically apply what you've learned over the course of a complete section. They are typically in the context of a real-world problem or situation.

 Warnings or important notes appear like this.

Get in Touch

Feedback from our readers is always welcome.

General feedback: Email feedback@packtpub.com and mention the book title in the subject of your message. If you have questions about any aspect of this book, please email us at questions@packtpub.com.

Errata: Although we have taken every care to ensure the accuracy of our content, mistakes do happen. If you have found a mistake in this book, we would be grateful if you would report this to us. Please visit www.packtpub.com/submit-errata, selecting your book, clicking on the Errata Submission Form link, and entering the details.

Piracy: If you come across any illegal copies of our works in any form on the Internet, we would be grateful if you would provide us with the location address or website name. Please contact us at copyright@packtpub.com with a link to the material.

If you are interested in becoming an author: If there is a topic that you have expertise in and you are interested in either writing or contributing to a book, please visit authors.packtpub.com.

Reviews

Please leave a review. Once you have read and used this book, why not leave a review on the site that you purchased it from? Potential readers can then see and use your unbiased opinion to make purchase decisions, we at Packt can understand what you think about our products, and our authors can see your feedback on their book. Thank you!

For more information about Packt, please visit packtpub.com.

 All the solutions to the activities are present in the *Appendix* section.

Basic Plotting in ggplot2

1

This chapter will cover basic concepts of ggplot2 and the Grammar of Graphics, using illustrative examples. You will generate solutions to problems of increasing complexity throughout the book. Lastly, you will master advanced plotting techniques, which will enable you to add more detail and increase the quality of your graphics.

In order to use ggplot2, you will first need to install R and RStudio. R is a programming language that is widely used for advanced modeling, statistical computing, and graphic production. R is considered the base package, while RStudio is a graphical interface (or IDE) that is based on R. Visualization is a very important aspect of data analysis, and it has its own underlying grammar (similar to the English language). There are many aspects of data analysis, and visualization is one of them. So, before we go further, let's discuss visualization in more detail.

By the end of this chapter, you will be able to:

- Distinguish between different kinds of variables
- Create simple plots and geometric objects, using qplot and ggplot2
- Determine the most appropriate visualization by comparing variables
- Utilize Grammar of Graphics concepts to improve plots in ggplot2

Introduction to ggplot2

ggplot2 is a visualization package in R. It was developed in 2005 and it uses the concept of the Grammar of Graphics to build a plot in layers and scales. This is the syntax used for the different components (aesthetics) of a geometric object. It also involves the grammatical rules for creating a visualization.

ggplot2 has grown in popularity over the years. It's a very powerful package, and its impressive scope has been enabled by the underlying grammar, which gives the user a very file level of control - making it perfect for a range of scenarios. Another great feature of ggplot 2 is that it is programmatic; hence, its visuals are reproducible. The ggplot2 package is open source, and its use is rapidly growing across various industries. Its visuals are flexible, professional, and can be created very quickly.

Read more about the top companies using R at https://www.listendata.com/2016/12/companies-using-r.html.

You can find out more about the role of a data scientist at https://www.innoarchitech.com/what-is-data-science-does-data-scientist-do/.

Similar Packages

Other visualization packages exist, such as matplotlib (in Python) and Tableau. The matplotlib and ggplot2 packages are equally popular, and they have similar features. Both are open source and widely used. Which one you would like to use may be a matter of preference. However, although both are programmatic and easy to use, since R was built with statisticians in mind, ggplot2 is considered to have more powerful graphics. More discussion on this topic can be found in the chapter later. Tableau is also very powerful, but it is limited in terms of statistical summaries and advanced data analytics. Tableau is not programmatic, and it is more memory intensive because it is completely interactive.

Excel has also been used for data analysis in the past, but it is not useful for processing the large amounts of data encountered in modern technology. It is interactive and not programmatic; hence, charts and graphs have to be made with interactivity and need to be updated every time more data is added. Packages such as ggplot2 are more powerful in that once the code is written, ggplot is independent of increases in the data, as long as the data structure is maintained. Also, ggplot2 provides a greater number of advanced plots that are not available in Excel.

Read more about Excel versus R at https://www.jessesadler.com/post/excel-vs-r/.

Read more about matplotlib versus R at http://pbpython.com/visualization-tools-1.html.

Read more about matplotlib versus ggplot at https://shiring.github.io/r_vs_python/2017/01/22/R_vs_Py_post.html.

The RStudio Workspace

So, before we go further, let's discuss visualization in more detail. Our first task is to load a dataset. To do so, we need to load certain packages in RStudio. Take a look at the screenshot of a typical RStudio layout, as follows:

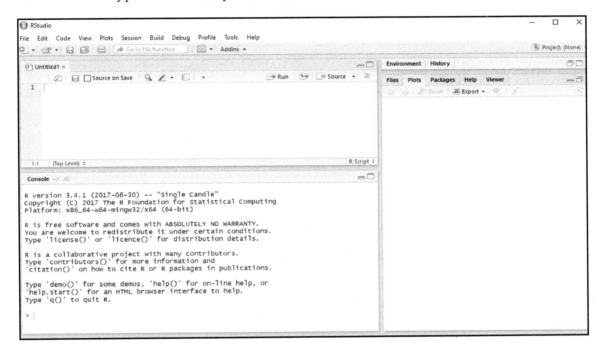

Loading and Exploring a Dataset Using R Functions

In this section, we'll load and explore a dataset using R functions. Before starting with the implementation, check the version by typing version in the console and checking the details, as follows:

```
> version
                    _
platform        x86_64-w64-mingw32
arch            x86_64
os              mingw32
system          x86_64, mingw32
status
major           3
minor           4.1
year            2017
month           06
day             30
svn rev         72865
language        R
version.string  R version 3.4.1 (2017-06-30)
nickname        Single Candle
```

Let's begin by following these steps:

1. Install the following packages and libraries:

   ```
   install.packages("ggplot2")
   install.packages("tibble")
   install.packages("dplyr")
   install.packages("Lock5Data")
   ```

2. Get the current working directory by using the getwd(".") command:

   ```
   [1] "C:/Users/admin/Documents/GitHub/Applied-DataVisualization-
   with-ggplot2-and-R"
   ```

3. Set the current working directory to Chapter 1 by using the following command:

   ```
   setwd("C:/Users/admin/Documents/GitHub/Applied-DataVisualization-
   with-ggplot2-and-R/Lesson1")
   ```

4. Use the require command to open the template_Lesson1.R file, which has the necessary libraries.

5. Read the following data file, provided in the data directory:

```
df_hum <- read.csv("data/historical-hourly-weather-
data/humidity.csv")
```

When we used `read.csv`, a structure called a data frame was created in R; which we are all familiar with it. Let's type some commands to get an overall impression of our data.

Let's retrieve some parameters of the dataset (such as the number of rows and columns) and display the different variables and their data types.

The following libraries have now been loaded:

- Graphical visualization package:

```
require("ggplot2")
```

- Build a data frame or list and some other useful commands:

```
require("tibble")
```

`require("dplyr")` - **Reference:** https://cran.r-project.org/web/ packages/dplyr/vignettes/dplyr.html.

- A built-in dataset package in R:

```
require("Lock5Data")
```

Reference: https://cran.r-project.org/web/packages/Lock5Data/ Lock5Data.pdf.

Use the following commands to determine the data frame details, as follows:

```
#Display the column names
colnames(df_hum)
```

Take a look at the output screenshot, as shown here:

```
colnames(df_hum)
 [1] "datetime"       "Vancouver"          "Portland"            "San.Francisco"   "Seattle"
 [6] "Los.Angeles"    "San.Diego"          "Las.Vegas"           "Phoenix"         "Albuquerque"
[11] "Denver"         "San.Antonio"        "Dallas"              "Houston"         "Kansas.City"
[16] "Minneapolis"    "Saint.Louis"        "Chicago"             "Nashville"       "Indianapolis"
[21] "Atlanta"        "Detroit"            "Jacksonville"        "Charlotte"       "Miami"
[26] "Pittsburgh"     "Toronto"            "Philadelphia"        "New.York"        "Montreal"
[31] "Boston"         "Beersheba"          "Tel.Aviv.District"   "Eilat"           "Haifa"
[36] "Nahariyya"      "Jerusalem"
```

Use the following command:

```
#Number of columns and rows
ndim(df_hum)
```

A summary of the data frame can be seen with the following code:

```
str(df_hum)
```

Take a look at the output screenshot, as shown here:

```
'data.frame':	45253 obs. of  37 variables:
 $ datetime      : Factor w/ 45253 levels "2012-10-01 12:00:00",..: 1 2 3 4 5 6 7 8 9 10 ...
 $ Vancouver     : num  NA 76 76 76 77 78 78 79 79 80 ...
 $ Portland      : num  NA 81 80 80 80 79 79 78 78 77 ...
 $ San.Francisco : num  NA 88 87 86 85 84 83 82 81 80 ...
 $ Seattle       : num  NA 81 80 80 79 79 78 77 77 76 ...
 $ Los.Angeles   : num  NA 88 88 88 88 88 88 88 88 88 ...
 $ San.Diego     : num  NA 82 81 81 81 80 80 80 79 79 ...
 $ Las.Vegas     : num  NA 22 21 21 21 21 21 20 20 20 ...
 $ Phoenix       : num  NA 23 23 23 23 24 24 24 25 25 ...
 $ Albuquerque   : num  NA 50 49 49 49 49 49 49 49 49 ...
 $ Denver        : num  NA 62 62 62 62 63 63 63 64 64 ...
```

The Main Concepts of ggplot2

ggplot2 is based on two main concepts: **geometric objects** and the **Grammar of Graphics**. The geometric objects in ggplot2 are the different visual structures that are used to visualize data. We will be going over them one by one. The Grammar of Graphics is the syntax that we use for the different aesthetics of a graph, such as the coordinate scale, the fonts, the color themes, and so on. ggplot2 uses a layered Grammar of Graphics concept, which allows us to build a plot in layers. We will work on some aspects of the Grammar of Graphics in this chapter, and will go into further details in the next chapter.

Types of Variables

Variables can be of different types and, sometimes, different software uses different names for the same variables. So, let's get familiar with the different kinds of variables that we will work with:

- **Continuous**: A continuous variable can take an infinite number of values, such as time or weight. They are of the numerical type.
- **Discrete**: A variable whose values are whole numbers (counts) is called a discrete variable. For example, the number of items bought by a customer in a supermarket is discrete.
- **Categorical**: The values of a categorical variable are selected from a small group of categories. Examples include gender (male or female) and make of car (Mazda, Hyundai, Toyota, and so on). Categorical variables can be further categorized into ordinal and nominal variables, as follows:
    - **Ordinal categorical variable**: A categorical variable whose categories can be meaningfully ordered is called ordinal. For example, credit grades (AA, A, B, C, D, and E) are ordinal.
    - **Nominal categorical variable**: It does not matter which way the categories are ordered in tabular or graphical displays of the data; all orderings are equally meaningful. An example would be different kinds of fruit (bananas, oranges, apples, and so on).
    - **Logical**: A logical variable can only take two values (T/F).

You can read more about variables at http://www.abs.gov.au/
websitedbs/a3121120.nsf/home/statistical+language+-
+what+are+variables.

The following table lists variables and the names that R uses for them; make sure to familiarize yourself with both nomenclatures.

The variable names used in R are as follows:

Variable Name	Short Form	Type
Numeric	num	Continuous/Discrete
Integer	int	Discrete
Logical	logical	logical
Factor	factor	Categorical
Character	chr	Categorical

 In R, whenever the factor data is listed, the number of levels is also given. A dataset can contain different kinds of variables, as discussed previously.

Exploring Datasets

In this section, we will use the built-in datasets to investigate the relationships between continuous variables, such as `temperature` and `airquality`. We'll explore and understand the datasets available in R.

Let's begin by executing the following steps:

1. Type `data()` in the command line to list the datasets available in R. You should see something like the following:

```
VADeaths          Death Rates in Virginia (1940)
WWWusage          Internet Usage per Minute
WorldPhones       The World's Telephones
ability.cov       Ability and Intelligence Tests
airmiles          Passenger Miles on Commercial US Airlines,
                  1937-1960
airquality        New York Air Quality Measurements
anscombe          Anscombe's Quartet of 'Identical' Simple
                  Linear Regressions
attenu            The Joyner-Boore Attenuation Data
```

2. Choose the following datasets: `mtcars`, `air quality`, `rock`, and `sleep`.

 The number of levels only applies to factor data.

3. List two variables of each type, the dataset names, and the other columns of this table.

4. To view the data type, use the `str` command (for example, `str(airquality)`).

Take a look at the following output screenshot:

```
'data.frame':    153 obs. of   6 variables:
 $ Ozone  : int  41 36 12 18 NA 28 23 19 8 NA ...
 $ Solar.R: int  190 118 149 313 NA NA 299 99 19 194 ...
 $ Wind   : num  7.4 8 12.6 11.5 14.3 14.9 8.6 13.8 20.1 8.6 ..
 $ Temp   : int  67 72 74 62 56 66 65 59 61 69 ...
 $ Month  : int  5 5 5 5 5 5 5 5 5 5 ...
 $ Day    : int  1 2 3 4 5 6 7 8 9 10 ...
```

5. After viewing the preceding datasets, fill in the following table. The first entry has been completed for you. The following table includes all variables of the types `num` and `int`:

Type	Variable Name	Dataset Name	Some Values	Number of Observations	Number of Levels
int	Area	rock	4990, 7002....	48	NA
int					
num					
num					
Factor					
Factor					

The outcome should be a completed table, similar to the following:

Type	Variable Name	Dataset Name	Some Values	Number of Observations	Number of Levels
int	Area	rock	4990, 7002....	48	NA
int	Ozone	airquality	41,36,12	153	NA
num	cyl	mtcars	6,4	32	NA
num	wind	airquality	7.4,8,12	153	NA
Factor	group	sleep	1,2	20	2
Factor	ID	sleep	1,2,3	20	10

More details about variables can be found at `http://www.statisticshowto.com/types-variables/`.

Making Your First Plot

The ggplot2 function `qplot` (quick plot) is similar to the basic `plot()` function from the R package. It has the following syntax: `qplot()`. It can be used to build and combine a range of useful graphs; however, it does not have the same flexibility as the `ggplot()` function.

Plotting with qplot and R

Suppose that we want to visualize some of the variables in the built-in datasets. A dataset can contain different kinds of variables, as discussed previously. Here, the climate data includes numerical data, such as the temperature, and categorical data, such as hot or cold. In order to visualize and correlate different kinds of data, we need to understand the nomenclature of the dataset. We'll load a data file and understand the structure of the dataset and its variables by using the qplot and R base package. Let's begin by executing the following steps:

1. Plot the `temperature` variable from the `airquality` dataset, with `hist(airquality$Temp)`.

`hist` is part of the built-in R graphics package.

Take a look at the following output screenshot:

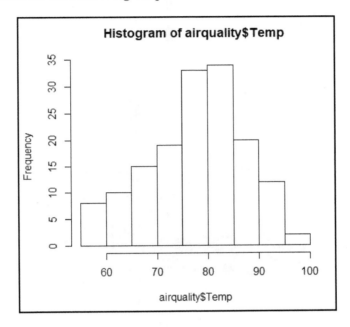

2. Use `qplot` (which is part of the ggplot2 package) to plot a graph, using the same variables.

3. Type the `qplot(airquality$Temp)` command to obtain the output, as shown in the following screenshot:

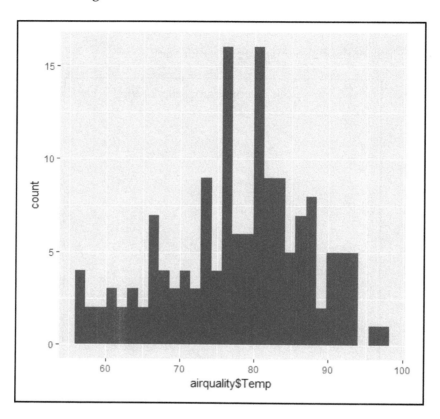

Analysis

The first plot was made in the built-in graphics package in R, while the second one was made using qplot, which is a plotting command in ggplot2. We can see that the two plots look very different. The plot is a histogram of the temperature.

We will discuss geometric objects later in this chapter, in order to understand the different types of histograms.

The built-in graphics package in R does not have a lot of features, so ggplot2 has become the package of choice. For the next exercises, we will continue to investigate making plots using ggplot2.

Geometric Objects

In your mathematics class, you likely studied geometry, examining different shapes and the characteristics of those shapes, such as area, perimeter, and other factors. The geometric objects in ggplot2 are visual structures that are used to visualize data. They can be lines, bars, points, and so on.

Geometric objects are constructed from datasets. Before we construct some geometric objects, let's examine some datasets to understand the different kinds of variables.

Analyzing Different Datasets

We all love to talk about the weather. So, let's work with some weather-related datasets. The datasets contain approximately five years' worth of high-temporal resolution (hourly measurements) data for various weather attributes, such as temperature, humidity, air pressure, and so on. We'll analyze and compare the humidity and weather datasets.

 Read more about weather datasets at: https://www.kaggle.com/selfishgene/historical-hourly-weather-data.

Let's begin by implementing the following steps:

1. Load the humidity dataset by using the following command:

```
df_hum <- read.csv("data/historical-hourly-weather-
data/humidity.csv")
```

2. Load the weather description dataset by using the following command:

```
df_desc <- read.csv("data/historical-hourly-weather-
data/weather_description.csv")
```

3. Compare the two datasets by using the str command.

The outcome will be the humidity levels of different cities, as follows:

```
$ datetime       : Factor w/ 45253 levels "2012-10-01 12:00:00",..: 1 2 3 4 5 6 7 8 9 10 ...
$ Vancouver      : num  NA 76 76 76 77 78 78 79 79 80 ...
$ Portland       : num  NA 81 80 80 79 79 78 78 77 ...
$ San.Francisco: num  NA 88 87 86 85 84 83 82 81 80 ...
$ Seattle        : num  NA 81 80 80 79 79 78 77 77 76 ...
$ Los.Angeles    : num  NA 88 88 88 88 88 88 88 88 88 ...
$ San.Diego      : num  NA 82 81 81 81 80 80 80 79 79 ...
$ Las.Vegas      : num  NA 22 21 21 21 21 21 21 20 20 ...
$ Phoenix        : num  NA 23 23 23 23 24 24 24 25 25 ...
$ Albuquerque    : num  NA 50 49 49 49 49 49 49 49 49 ...
```

The weather descriptions of different cities are shown as follows:

```
> glimpse(df_desc)
Observations: 44,459
Variables: 4
$ x               <int> 2, 3, 4, 5, 6, 7, 8, 9, 10, 11, 12, 13, 14, 15, 16, 17, 18, 19, 20, 21, 22, 23, 24, 2...
$ Vancouver       <fct> mist, Cloudy, Cloudy, Cloudy, Cloudy, Cloudy, Cloudy, Cloudy, Cloudy, Cloudy, Cloudy,...
$ Seattle         <fct> clear, clear, clear, clear, clear, clear, clear, clear, clear, clear, Cloudy, Cloudy,...
$ San.Francisco <fct> raining, clear, clear, clear, clear, clear, clear, clear, clear, clear, clear, clear,...
> |
```

The different geometric objects that we will be working with in this chapter are as follows:

One-dimensional objects are used to understand and visualize the characteristics of a single variable, as follows:

- Histogram
- Bar chart

Two-dimensional objects are used to visualize the relationship between two variables, as follows:

- Bar chart
- Boxplot
- Line chart
- Scatter plot

Although geometric objects are also used in base R, they don't follow the structure of the Grammar of Graphics and have different naming conventions, as compared to ggplot2. This is an important distinction, which we will look at in detail later.

Histograms

Histograms are used to group and represent numerical (continuous) variables.
For example, you may want to know the distribution of voters' ages in an election.
A histogram is often confused with a bar chart; however, a bar chart is more general, and
we will cover those later. In a histogram, a continuous variable is grouped into bins of
specific sizes and the bins have a range that covers the maximum and minimum of the
variable in question.

Histograms can be classified as follows:

- **Unimodal:** A distribution with a single maximum or mode; for example,
  a normal distribution:
    - A normal distribution (or a bell-shaped curve) is symmetrical. An
      example is the grade distribution of students in a class. A
      unimodal distribution may or may not be symmetrical. It can be
      positively or negatively skewed, as well.
    - Positively or negatively skewed (also known as right-skewed or
      left-skewed): Skewness is a measure of the asymmetry of the
      probability distribution of a real-valued random variable about its
      mean. The skewness value can be positive, negative, or undefined.
    - A left-skewed distribution has a long tail to the left while a right-
      skewed distribution has a long tail to the right. An example of a
      right-skewed distribution might be the US household income, with
      a long tail of higher-income groups.

- **Bimodal:** Bimodal distribution resembles the back of a two-humped camel. It
  shows the outcomes of two processes, with different distributions that are
  combined into one set of data. For example, you might expect to see a bimodal
  distribution in the height distribution of an entire population. There would be a
  peak around the average height of a man, and a peak around the typical height of
  a woman.

- **Unitary distribution**: This distribution follows a uniform pattern that has approximately the same number of values in each group. In the real world, one can only find approximately uniform distributions. An example is the speed of a car versus time if moving at constant speed (zero acceleration), or the uniform distribution of heat in a microwave:

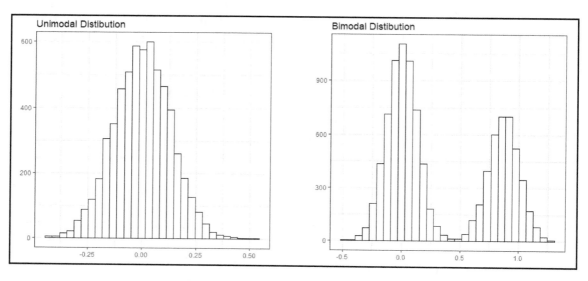

Let's take a look at another image:

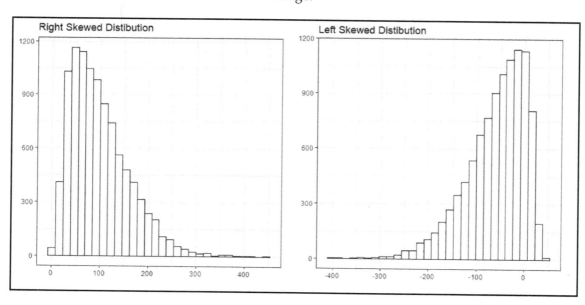

It's important to study the shapes of distributions, as they can reveal a lot about the nature of data. We will see some real-world examples of histograms in the datasets that we will explore.

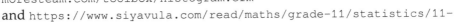

To learn more about bar charts and histograms, visit `https://www2.le.ac.uk/offices/ld/resources/numericaldata/histograms`.

You can read more about the shapes of histograms at `https://www.moresteam.com/toolbox/histogram.cfm` and `https://www.siyavula.com/read/maths/grade-11/statistics/11-statistics-05`.

Find out more about normal distributions at `http://onlinestatbook.com/2/normal_distribution/history_normal.html`.

You will find more real-world examples at `https://stats.stackexchange.com/questions/33776/real-life-examples-of-common-distributions`.

We discussed the different kinds of geometric objects that we will be working on, and we created our fist plot using two different methods (`qplot` and `hist`). Now, let's use another command: `ggplot`. We will use the humidity data that we loaded previously.

As seen in the preceding section, we can create a default histogram by using one of the commands in the base R package: `hist`. This is seen in the following command:

```
hist(df_hum$Vancouver)
```

The default histogram that will be created is as follows:

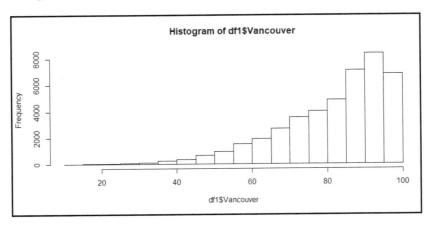

Creating a Histogram Using qplot and ggplot

In this section, we want to visualize the humidity distribution for the city of Vancouver. We'll create a histogram for humidity data using qplot and ggplot.

Let's begin by implementing the following steps:

1. Create a plot with RStudio by using the following command:
   `qplot(df_hum$Vancouver):`

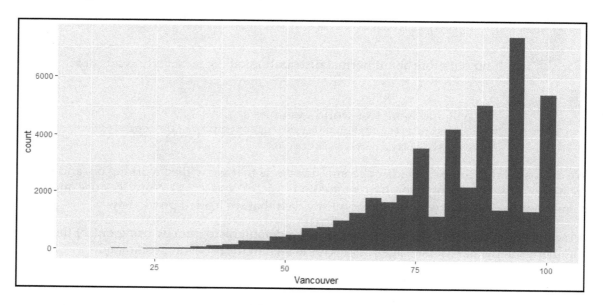

2. Use ggplot to create the same plot using the following command:

   `ggplot(df_hum,aes(x=Vancouver))`

   This command does not do anything; ggplot2 requires the name of the object that we wish to make. To make a histogram, we have to specify the geom type (in other words, a histogram). `aes` stands for aesthetics, or the quantities that get plotted on the *x*- and *y*-axes, and their qualities. We will work on changing the aesthetics later, in order to visualize the plot more effectively.

Notice that there are some warning messages, as follows:

```
'stat_bin()' using 'bins = 30'. Pick better value with 'binwidth'.
Warning message:
Removed 1826 rows containing non-finite values (stat_bin).
```

You can ignore these messages; ggplot automatically detects and removes null or NA values.

3. Obtain the histogram with `ggplot` by using the following command:

```
ggplot (df_hum, aes(x=Vancouver)) + geom_histogram()
```

You'll see the following output:

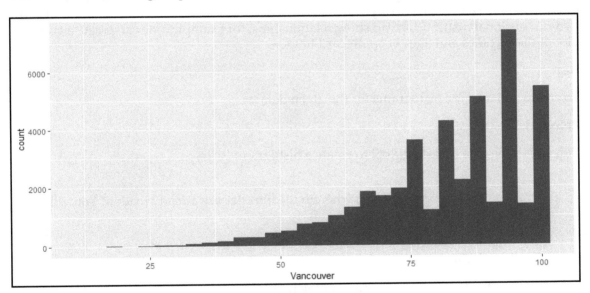

Here's the output code:

```
require("ggplot2")
require("tibble")
#Load a data file - Read the Humidity Data
df_hum <- read.csv("data/historical-hourly-weather-data/humidity.csv")
#Display the summary
str(df_hum)
qplot(df_hum$Vancouver)
ggplot(df_hum, aes(x=Vancouver)) + geom_histogram()
```

Refer to the complete code at `https://goo.gl/tu7t4y`.

In order for ggplot to work, you will need to specify the geometric object. Note that the column name should not be enclosed in strings.

Activity: Creating a Histogram and Explaining its Features

Scenario

Histograms are useful when you want to find the peak and spread in a distribution. For example, suppose that a company wants to see what its client age distribution looks like. A two-dimensional distribution can show relationships; for example, one can create a scatter plot of the incomes and ages of credit card holders.

Aim

To create and analyze histograms for the given dataset.

Prerequisites

You should be able to use ggplot2 to create a histogram.

This is an empty code, wherein the libraries are already loaded. You will be writing your code here.

Steps for Completion

1. Use the template code and load the required datasets.
2. Create the histogram for two cities.
3. Analyze and compare two histograms to determine the point of difference.

Outcome

Two histograms should be created and compared. The complete code is as follows:

```
df_t <- read.csv("data/historical-hourly-weather-data/temperature.csv")
ggplot(df_t,aes(x=Vancouver))+geom_histogram()
ggplot(df_t,aes(x=Miami))+geom_histogram()
```

Refer to the complete code at `https://goo.gl/tu7t4y`.

Take a look at the following output histogram:

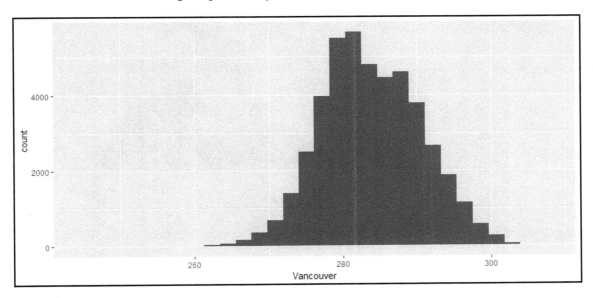

From the preceding plot, we can determine the following information:

- Vancouver's maximum temperature is around 280.
- It ranges between 260 and 300.
- It's a right-skewed distribution.

Take a look at the following output histogram:

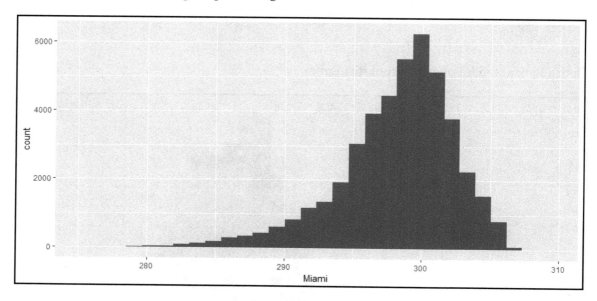

From the preceding plot, we can determine the following information:

- Miami's maximum temperature is around 300
- It ranges between 280 and 308
- It's a left-skewed distribution

Differences

1. Miami's temperature plot is skewed to the right, while Vancouver's is to the left.
2. The maximum temperature is higher for Miami.

Creating Bar Charts

Bar charts are more general than histograms, and they can represent both discrete and continuous data. They can even be used to represent categorical variables. A bar chart uses a horizontal or vertical rectangular bar that levels of at an appropriate level. A bar chart can be used to represent various quantities, such as frequency counts and percentages.

We will use the weather description data to create a bar chart. To create a bar chart, the geometric object used is `geom_bar()`.

The syntax is as follows:

```
ggplot(....) + geom_bar(...)
```

If we use the `glimpse` or `str` command to view the weather data, we will get the following results:

```
> glimpse(df_desc)
Observations: 44,459
Variables: 4
$ x             <int> 2, 3, 4, 5, 6, 7, 8, 9, 10, 11, 12, 13, 14, 15, 16, 17, 18, 19, 20, 21, 22, 23, 24, 2...
$ Vancouver     <fct> mist, Cloudy, Cloudy, Cloudy, Cloudy, Cloudy, Cloudy, Cloudy, Cloudy, Cloudy, Cloudy,...
$ Seattle       <fct> clear, clear, clear, clear, clear, clear, clear, clear, clear, clear, Cloudy, Cloudy,...
$ San.Francisco <fct> raining, clear, clear, clear, clear, clear, clear, clear, clear, clear, clear, clear,...
> |
```

 You cannot use a histogram for a categorical type of variable.

Creating a One-Dimensional Bar Chart

Use the `ggplot(df_vanc,aes(x=Vancouver)) + geom_bar()` command to obtain the following chart:

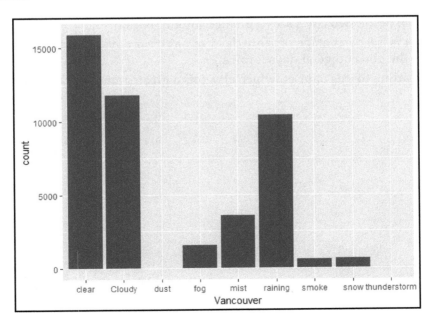

Observations

Vancouver has clear weather, for the most part. It rained about 10,000 times for the dataset provided. Snowy periods are much less frequent.

We will now perform two exercises, creating a one-dimensional bar chart and a two-dimensional bar chart. A one-dimensional bar chart can give us the **counts** or **frequency** of a given variable. A two-dimensional bar chart can give us the relationship between the variables.

In this section, we'll count the number of times each type of weather occurs in Seattle and compare it to Vancouver.

Let's begin by following these steps:

1. Use ggplot2 and `geom_bar` in conjunction to create the bar chart.
2. Use the data frame that we just created, but with Seattle instead of Vancouver, as follows:

   ```
   ggplot(df_vanc,aes(x=Seattle)) + geom_bar()
   ```

3. Now, compare the two bar charts and answer the following questions:

   - Approximately how many times was Vancouver cloudy? (Round to 2 significant figures.)
   - Which of the two cities sees a greater amount of rain?
   - What is the percentage of rainy days versus clear days? (Add the two counts and give the percentage of days it rains.)
   - According to this dataset, which city gets a greater amount of snow?

You should see the following output:

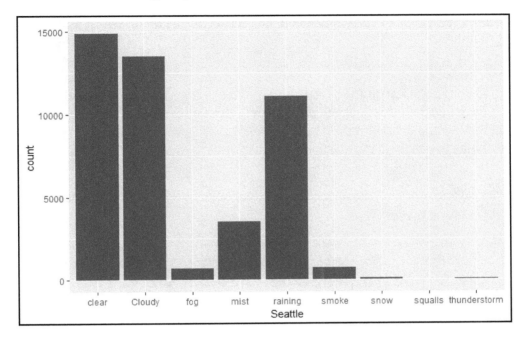

  Refer to the complete code at `https://goo.gl/tu7t4y`.

Answers

- Vancouver was cloudy 13,000 times. (Note that 12,000 is also acceptable.)
- Seattle sees a greater amount of rain.

    It rained on approximately 40% of the days.

- Vancouver gets a greater amount of snow.

A two-dimensional bar chart can be used to plot the sum of a continuous variable versus a categorical or discrete variable. For example, you might want to plot the total amount of rainfall in different weather conditions, or the total amount of sales in different months.

Creating a Two-Dimensional Bar Chart

In this section, we'll create a two-dimensional bar chart for the total sales of a company in different months.

Let's begin by following these steps:

1. Load the data. Add the line `require (Lock5Data)` into your code. You should have installed this package previously.
2. Review the data with the `glimpse(RetailSales)` command.
3. Plot a graph of `Sales` versus `Month`.

> Here, `Month` is a categorical variable, while `Sales` is a continuous variable of the type `<dbl>`.

4. Use `ggplot + geom_bar(..)` to plot this data, as follows:

```
ggplot(RetailSales,aes(x=Month,y=Sales)) +
geom_bar(stat="identity")
```

A screenshot of the expected outcome is as follows:

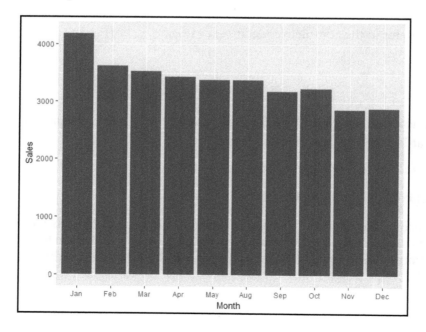

Analyzing and Creating Boxplots

A **boxplot** (also known as a box and whisker diagram) is a standard way of displaying the distribution of data based on a file-number summary: **minimum, first quartile, median, third quartile**, and **maximum**. Boxplots can represent how a continuous variable is distributed for different categories; one of the axes will be a categorical variable, while the other will be a continuous variable. In the default boxplot, the central rectangle spans the first quartile to the third quartile (called the **interquartile** range, or **IQR**). A segment inside of the rectangle shows the median, and the lines (**whiskers**) above and below the box indicate the locations of the minimum and maximum, as shown in the following diagram:

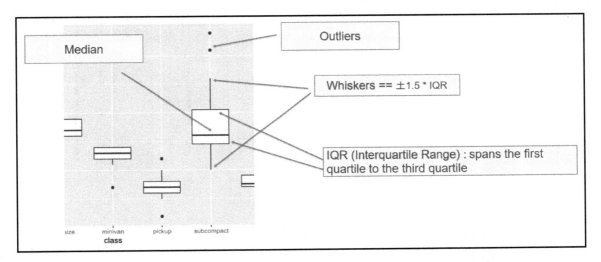

The upper whisker extends from the hinge to the largest and smallest values of ± 1.5 * IQR from the hinge. Here, we can see the humidity data as a function of the month. Data beyond the end of the whiskers are called outliers, and are represented as circles, as seen in the following chart:

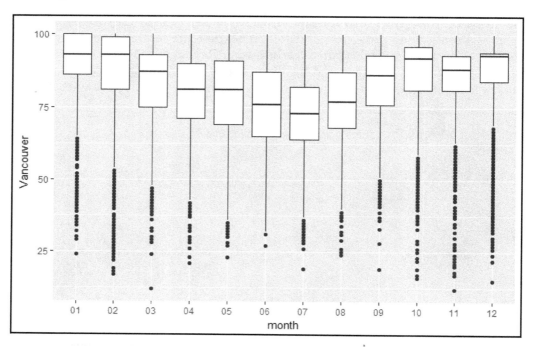

You'll get the preceding chart by using the following code:

```
ggplot(df_hum, aes(x=month, y=Vancouver)) + geom_boxplot()
```

 Read more about boxplots at: http://ggplot2.tidyverse.org/ reference/geom_boxplot.html.

Creating a Boxplot for a Given Dataset

In this section, we'll create a boxplot for monthly temperature data for Seattle and San Francisco, and compare the two (given two points).

Let's begin by implementing the following steps:

1. Create the two boxplots.
2. Display them side by side in your Word document.
3. Provide two points of comparison between the two. You can comment on how the medians compare, how uniform the distributions look, the maximum and minimum humidity, and so on.

 Refer to the complete code at `https://goo.gl/tu7t4y`.

The following observations can be noted:

The humidity is more uniform for San Francisco:

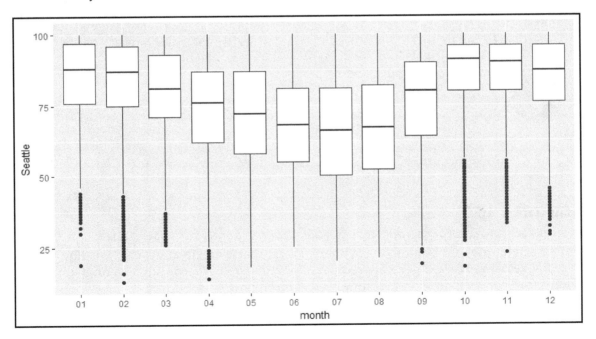

The median humidity for San Francisco is about 75:

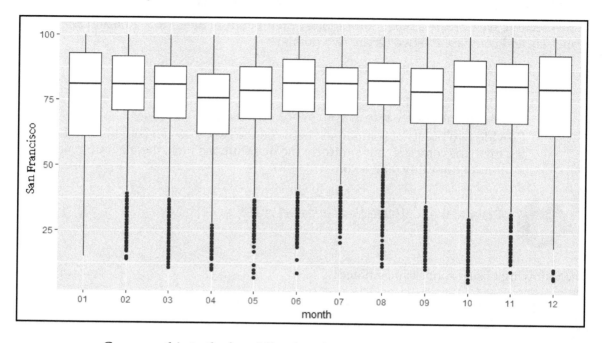

 Compare this to the humidity data for Seattle and San Francisco on the following websites (scroll down and look for the humidity plots). You should see a similar trend:

```
https://weather-and-climate.com/average-monthly-Rainfall-
Temperature-Sunshine,Seattle,United-States-of-America
```

```
https://weather-and-climate.com/average-monthly-Rainfall-
Temperature-Sunshine,San-Francisco,United-States-of-America
```

Scatter Plots

A scatter plot shows the relationship between two continuous variables. Let's create a scatter plot of distance versus time for a car that is accelerating and traveling with an initial velocity. We will generate some random time points according to a function. The relationship between distance and time for a speeding car is as follows:

$$x = x_0 + v_0 t + 0.5 a t^2$$

We can draw a scatter plot to show the relationship between distance and time with the following code:

```
ggplot(df,aes(x=time,y=distance)) + geom_point()
```

We can see a positive correlation, meaning that as time increases, distance increases. Take a look at the following code:

```
a=3.4
v0=27
time <- runif(50, min=0, max=200)
distance <- sapply(time, function(x) v0*x + 0.5*a*x^2)
df <- data.frame(time,distance)
ggplot(df,aes(x=time,y=distance)) + geom_point()
```

The outcome is a positive correlation: as time increases, distance increases:

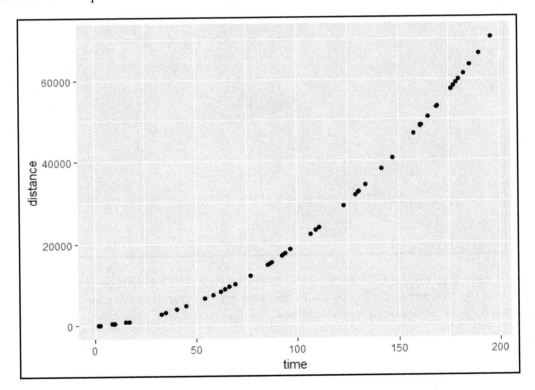

The correlation can also be zero (for no relationship) or negative (as *x* increases, *y* decreases).

Line Charts

A line chart shows the relationship between two variables; it is similar to a scatter plot, but the points are connected by line segments. One difference between the usage of a scatter plot and a line chart is that, typically, it's more meaningful to use the line chart if the variable being plotted on the x-axis has a one-to-one relationship with the variable being plotted on the y-axis. A line chart should be used when you have enough data points, so that a smooth line is meaningful to see a functional dependence:

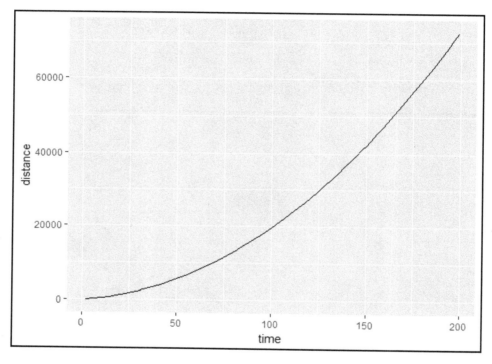

We could have also used a line chart for the previous plot. The advantage of using a line chart is that the discrete nature goes away and you can see trends more easily, while the functional form is more effectively visualized.

If there is more than one y value for a given x, the data needs to be grouped by the x value; then, one can show the features of interest from the grouped data, such as the mean, median, maximum, minimum, and so on. We will use grouping in the next section.

Creating a Line Chart

In this section, we'll create a line chart to plot the mean humidity against the month. Lets's begin by implementing the following steps:

1. Convert the months into numerical integers, as follows:

```
df_hum$monthn <- as.numeric(df_hum$month)
```

2. Group the humidity by month and remove NAs, as follows:

```
gp1 <- group_by(df_hum,monthn)
```

3. Create a summary of the group using the mean and median.
4. Now, use the `geom_line()` command to plot the line chart (refer to the code).

The following plots are obtained:

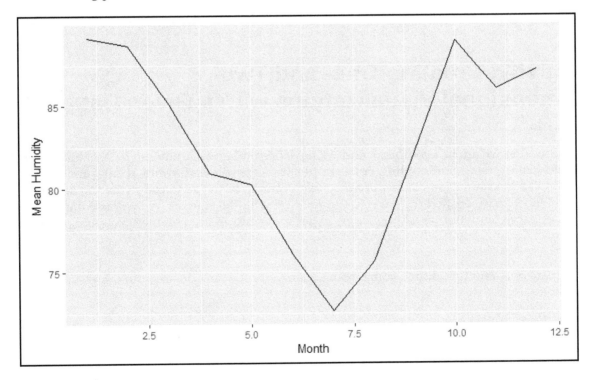

Refer to the complete code at `https://goo.gl/tu7t4y`.

Take a look at the output line chart:

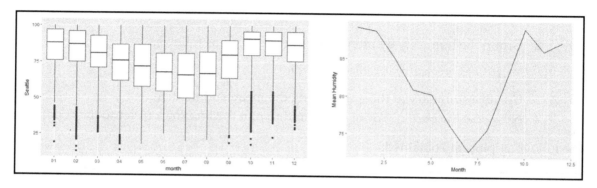

Activity: Creating One- and Two-Dimensional Visualizations with a Given Dataset

Scenario

Suppose that we are in a company, and we have been given an unknown dataset and would like to create similar plots. For example, we have some educational data, and we would like to know what courses are the most popular, or the gender distribution among students, or how satisfied the parents/students are with the courses. We will use the new dataset, along with our own knowledge, to get some information on the preceding points.

Aim

To create one- and two-dimensional visualizations for the new dataset and the given variables.

Steps for Completion

1. Load the datasets.
2. Choose the appropriate visualization.
3. Create the desired 1D visualization.
4. Create two-dimensional boxplots or scatter plots and note your observations.

Outcome

Three one-dimensional plots and three two-dimensional plots should be created, with the following axes (count versus topic) and observations. (Note that the students may provide different observations, so the instructor should verify the answers. The following observations are just examples.)

 Refer to the complete code at `https://goo.gl/tu7t4y`.

One-Dimensional Plots

This visual was chosen because **Topic** is a categorical variable, and I wanted to see the frequency of each topic:

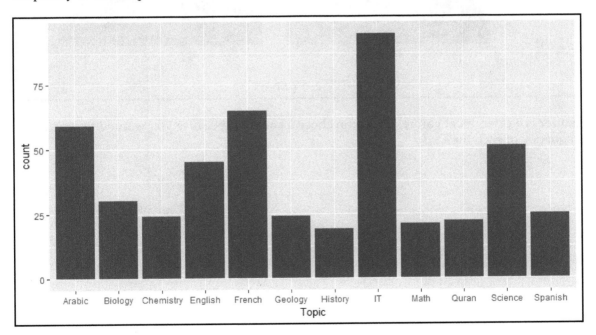

Observation

You can see that IT is the most popular subject:

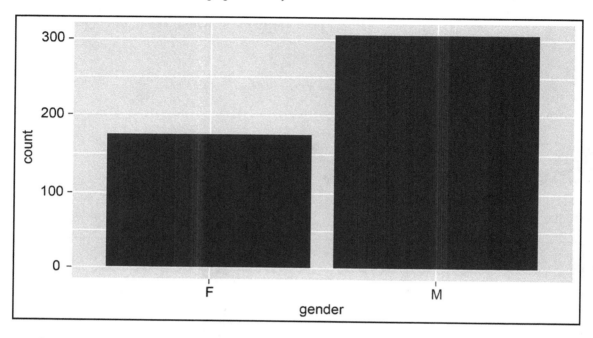

gender is a categorical variable; you can chose a bar chart because you wanted to see the frequency of each topic.

Observation

You can observe that more males are registered in this institute from the following histogram:

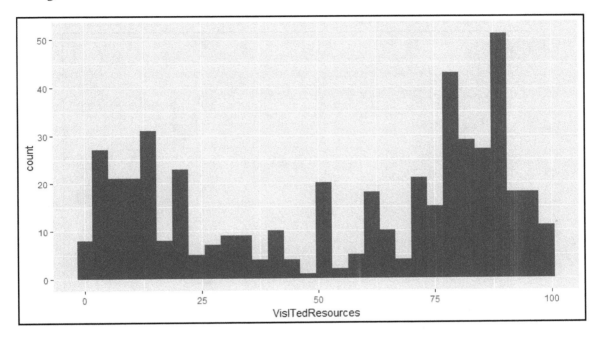

VisitedResources is **numerical**, so you can choose a **histogram** to visualize it.

Observation

It's a **bimodal** histogram with two peaks, around 12 and 85.

Two-Dimensional Plots

Take a look at the following 2D plots:

Plot 1:

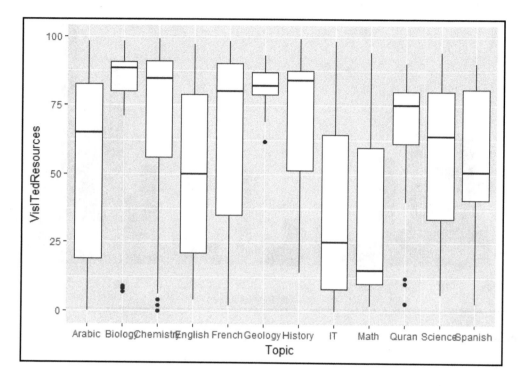

Plot 2:

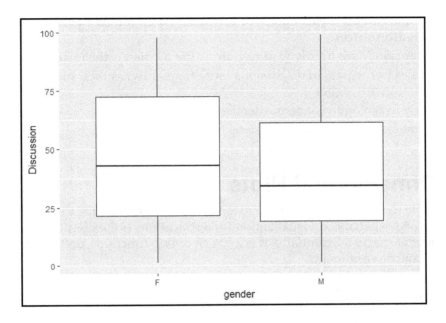

Plot 3:

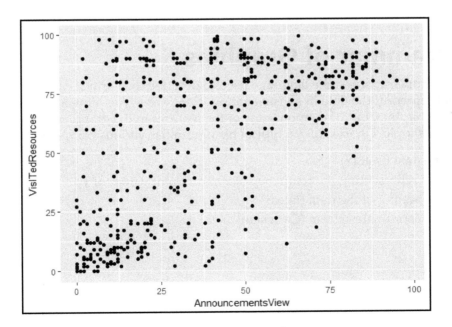

Observations

- I see that there is a weak positive correlation between **AnnouncementsView** and **VisitedResources**.
- Students in Math hardly visit resources; the median is the lowest, at about 12.5.
- Females participate in discussions more frequently, as their median and maximum are higher.
- People in Biology visit resources the most.
- The median number of discussions for females is 37.5.

Three-Dimensional Plots

It is also possible to plot using three-dimensional vectors. This creates a three-dimensional plot, which provides enhanced visualization for applications (for example, displaying three-dimensional spaces). Essentially, it is a graph of two functions, embedded into a three-dimensional environment.

 Read more about three-dimensional plots at: https://octave.org/doc/ v4.2.0/Three_002dDimensional-Plots.html.

The Grammar of Graphics

The Grammar of Graphics is the language used to describe the various components of a graphic that represent the data in a visualization. Here, we will explore a few aspects of the Grammar of Graphics, building upon some of the features in the graphics that we created in the previous topic. For example, a typical histogram has various components, as follows:

- The data itself (x)
- Bars representing the frequency of x at different values of x
- The scaling of the data (linear)
- The coordinate system (Cartesian)

All of these aspects are part of the Grammar of Graphics, and we will change these aspects to provide better visualization. In this chapter, we will work with some of the aspects; we will explore them further in the next chapter.

 Read more about the Grammar of Graphics at `https://cfss.uchicago.edu/dataviz_grammar_of_graphics.html`.

Rebinning

In a histogram, data is grouped into intervals, or ranges of values, called bins. ggplot has a certain number of bins by default, but the default may not be the best choice every time. Having too many bins in a histogram might not reveal the shape of the distribution, while having too few bins might distort the distribution. It is sometimes necessary to rebin a histogram, in order to get a smooth distribution.

Analyzing Various Histograms

Let's use the humidity data and the first plot that we created. It looks like the humidity values are discrete, which is why you can see discrete peaks in the data. In this section, we'll analyze the differences between unbinned and binned histograms.

Let's begin by implementing the following steps:

1. Choosing a different type of binning can make the distribution more continuous; use the following code:

```
ggplot(df_hum,aes(x=Vancouver))+geom_histogram(bins=15)
```

You'll get the following output. Graph 1:

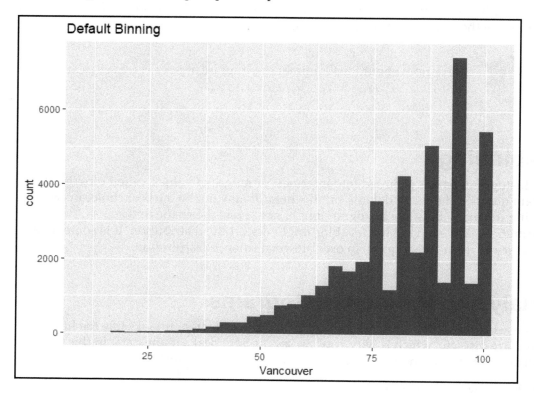

Graph 2:

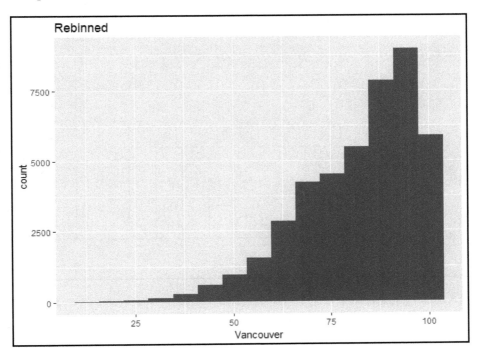

 Choosing a different type of binning can make the distribution more continuous, and one can then better understand the distribution shape. We will now build upon the graph, changing some features and adding more layers.

2. Change the fill color to white by using the following command:

```
ggplot(df_hum,aes(x=Vancouver))+geom_histogram(bins=15,fill="white"
,color=1)
```

3. Add a title to the histogram by using the following command:

```
+ggtitle("Humidity for Vancouver city")
```

4. Change the x-axis label and label sizes, as follows:

```
+xlab("Humidity")+theme(axis.text.x=element_text(size =
12),axis.text.y=element_text(size=12))
```

You should see the following output:

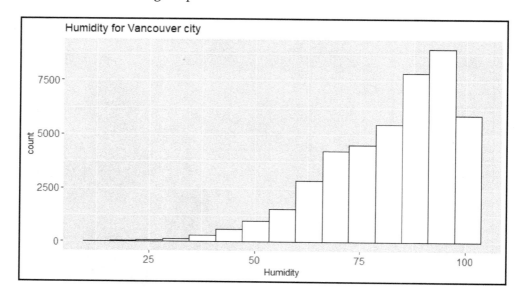

The full command should look as follows:

```
ggplot(df_hum,aes(x=Vancouver))+geom_histogram(bins=15,fi
ll="white",color=1)+ggtitle("Humidity for Vancouver
city")+xlab("Humidity")+theme(axis.text.x=element_text(si
ze= 12),axis.text.y=element_text(size=12))
```

We can see that the second plot is a visual improvement, due to the following factors:

- There is a title
- The font sizes are visible
- The histogram looks more professional in white

To see what else can be changed, type ?theme.

Changing Boxplot Defaults Using the Grammar of Graphics

In this section, we'll use the Grammar of Graphics to change defaults and create a better visualization.

Let's begin by implementing the following steps:

1. Use the humidity data to create the same boxplot seen in the previous section, for plotting monthly data.
2. Change the x- and y-axis labels appropriately (the x-axis is the month and the y-axis is the humidity).
3. Type ?geom_boxplot in the command line, then look for the aesthetics, including the color and the fill color.
4. Change the color to black and the fill color to green (try numbers from 1-6).
5. Type ?theme to find out how to change the label size to 15. Change the *x*- and *y*-axis titles to size 15 and the color to red.

The outcome will be the complete code and the graphic with the correct changes:

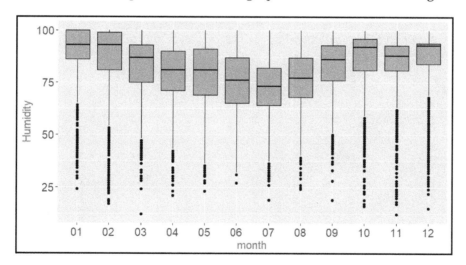

 Refer to the complete code at https://goo.gl/tu7t4y.

Activity: Improving the Default Visualization

Scenario

In the previous activity, you made a judicious choice of a geometric object (bar chart or histogram) for a given variable. In this activity, you will see how to improve a visualization. If you are producing plots to look at privately, you might be okay using the default settings. However, when you are creating plots for publication or giving a presentation, or if your company requires a certain theme, you will need to produce more professional plots that adhere to certain visualization rules and guidelines. This activity will help you to improve visuals and create a more professional plot.

Aim

To create improved visualizations by using the Grammar of Graphics.

Steps for Completion

1. Create two of the plots from the previous activity.
2. Use the Grammar of Graphics to improve your graphics by layering upon the base graphic.

 Refer to the complete code at `https://goo.gl/tu7t4y`.

Take a look at the following output, histogram 1:

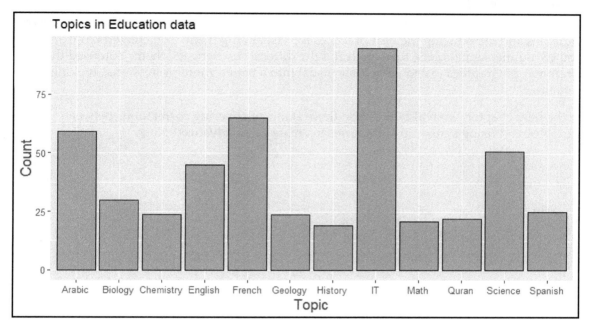

Histogram 2:

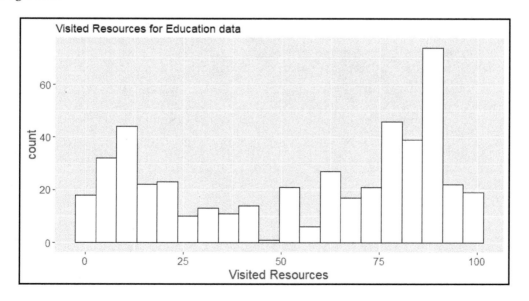

Summary

In this chapter, we covered the basics of ggplot2, distinguishing between different types of variables and introducing the best practices for visualizing them. You created basic one- and two-dimensional plots, then analyzed the differences between them. You used the Grammar of Graphics to change a basic visual into a better, more professional-looking visual.

In the next chapter, we will build upon these skills, uncovering correlations between variables and using statistical summaries to create more advanced plots.

2

Grammar of Graphics and Visual Components

In this chapter, we will explore the concept of the Grammar of Graphics in detail and use it to customize graphs to create better visualizations.

We need to customize graphs because default graphs may have fonts that are not visible in a presentation or document, or have scales that do not convey much information about the data. Sometimes, a company may require a uniform style for all their graphs to distinguish themselves, in which case, you would need to define and use the same style for all graphs. We may also need to split data into different subsets in order to understand it in greater detail. This chapter will explore these aspects in detail and explain how to change the default structure of a graph.

By the end of this chapter, you will be able to:

- Apply the Grammar of Graphics techniques to layers, scales, and coordinates
- Utilize faceting to make multiplots and divide data into subplots
- Utilize colors in plots effectively
- Modify the appearance of graphs by implementing themes
- Create statistical summaries by grouping data

More on the Grammar of Graphics

The Grammar of Graphics is the language used to describe the various components of a graphic that represent data in a visualization. In this topic, you will learn more about the Grammar of Graphics and will use it to make plots. You will e-encounter some of the Grammar of Graphics terms used in the previous chapter.

We will now break down the Grammar of Graphics language, in order to understand the terms in greater detail.

Layers

In ggplot2, every plot is built up as a layer. Layers are made up of geometric objects (*geoms*), their statistical transformations (*stats*), and their thematic aspects. Hence, each plot can be thought of as a separate variable, in and of itself. Aesthetic mappings, defined with `aes()`, describe how variables are mapped to visual properties, or aesthetics. The following diagram depicts the use of the `df` and `aes` functions:

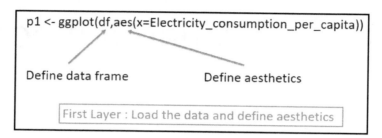

Let's look at an example. We will use the `gapminder` dataset. You can see the available variables in the following snippet. The dataset has different variables for different countries; for example, `gdp_per_capita`, `Electricity_consumption_per_capita`, and so on:

```
Observations: 1,512
Variables: 10
$ X                                  <int> 0, 1, 2, 3, 4, 5, 6, 7, 8, 9, 10, 11, 1...
$ Country                            <fct> Brazil, Brazil, Brazil, Brazil, Brazil,...
$ Year                               <int> 1800, 1801, 1802, 1803, 1804, 1805, 180...
$ gdp_per_capita                     <int> 1109, 1109, 1109, 1109, 1109, 1110, 111...
$ Electricity_consumption_per_capita <dbl> NA, NA, NA, NA, NA, NA, NA, NA, NA, NA,...
$ under5mortality                    <dbl> 417.44, 417.44, 417.44, 417.44, 417.44,...
$ Poverty                            <dbl> NA, NA, NA, NA, NA, NA, NA, NA, NA, NA,...
$ BMI_male                           <dbl> NA, NA, NA, NA, NA, NA, NA, NA, NA, NA,...
$ BMI_female                         <dbl> NA, NA, NA, NA, NA, NA, NA, NA, NA, NA,...
$ Year_as_fac                        <fct> 1800, 1801, 1802, 1803, 1804, 1805, 180...
```

Let's build a histogram for electricity consumption per capita. We will not be analyzing this histogram, so don't worry about the features:

- The first layer will define the aesthetics, or the variables, that we want to look at:

  ```
  aes p1 <- ggplot (df,aes (x=Electricity_consumption_per_capita)).
  ```

- The second layer will define the geometric object:

  ```
  p2 <- p1+geom_histogram ().
  ```

- In this layer, we will rebin the histogram:

```
p3 <- p1+geom_histogram(bins=15).
```

- We will then plot the following histogram:

```
p3.
```

You'll get the following histogram:

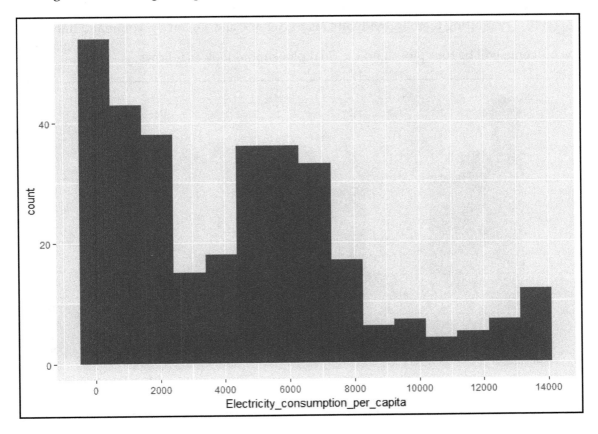

Using More Layers to Customize a Histogram

In this section, we'll use layers to customize a histogram.

Let's begin by implementing the following steps:

1. Plot the two preceding histograms.
2. Change the *x*-axis title: Add another layer to change the *x*-axis title (remove the _ in the variable name), and save it in a plot (p4).
3. Try plotting them individually (as p1, p2, p3, and p4) on the command line.

The outcome will be four plots, and the final plot should look as follows:

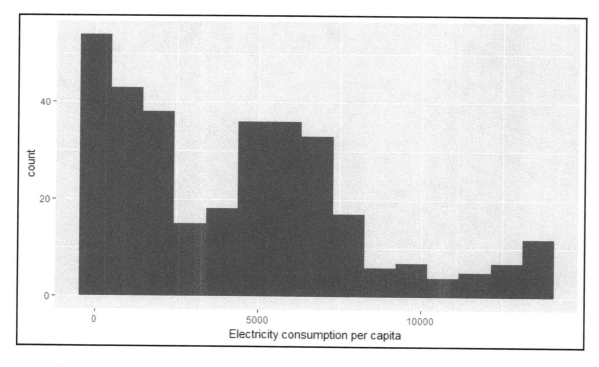

Scales

Scales map values in a data space to values in an aesthetic space, whether the value is a color, shape, or size. Scales are used to change legends or axes, providing inverse mapping and enabling us to understand the data from the graphic itself. In the previous example, when we plotted the histogram, ggplot applied a default scale, in order to describe the x- and y-axes. However, we can modify that scale.

To modify scales, the following commands are used:

- **Continuous variables**: `scale_x_continuous` (x-axis), `scale_y_continuous` (y-axis).
- **Discrete variables**: `scale_x_discrete` (x-axis), `scale_y_discrete` (y-axis).

Some elements that are commonly changed are as follows:

- **name:** The first argument gives the axis or legend title.
- **limits:** The minimum and maximum of the scale.
- **breaks:** The points along the scale where labels should appear.
- **labels:** The labels that appear at each break.

Let's use these commands in the following section.

Using Scales to Analyze a Dataset

In this section, we'll explore some of the options available in `scale_x_continuous` and `scale_x_discrete`.

Let's begin by implementing the following steps:

1. Use the same dataset from the previous exercise, and plot the `gdp_per_capita` as a histogram.

2. Plot p1, as follows:

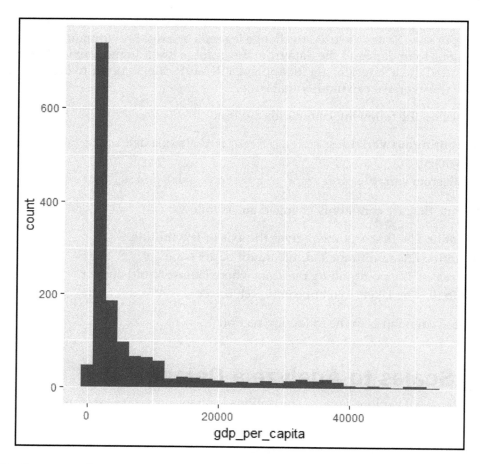

3. Can you tell where the maximum occurs? No; it's too approximate. We need a finer method of labeling.
4. Study and view the options in `scale_x_continuous`. (Use the `?scale_x_continuous` command on the command line in order to see the options.)
5. Add the `scale_x_continuous` layer:

```
breaks=seq (0,40000,4000))
```

This command defines a range from 0-40,000, with breaks of 4,000.

You can now identify the maximum more easily. What is the maximum GDP per capita? What type of histogram is this?

Take a look at the output histogram following:

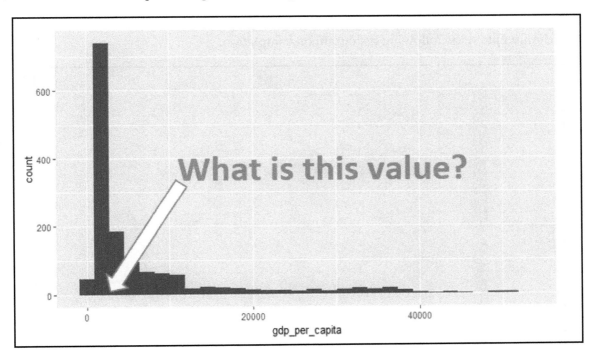

Let's take a look at the following image:

```
p1 <- ggplot(df,aes(x=gdp_per_capita))
p2 <- p1+geom_histogram()
p2
#where does the maximum occur? We need to have a finer labelling to answer
#the question
p2 + scale_x_continuous(breaks=seq(0,40000,4000) )
```

Since it's a continuous variable, we use `scale_x_continuous` to set breaks.

The object breaks is a vector defined by the command `seq(0,40000,4000)`. It breaks the ticks in steps of 4,000, from 0-40,000.

 Refer to the complete code at `https://goo.gl/RheL2G`.

You should obtain the following histogram on completion:

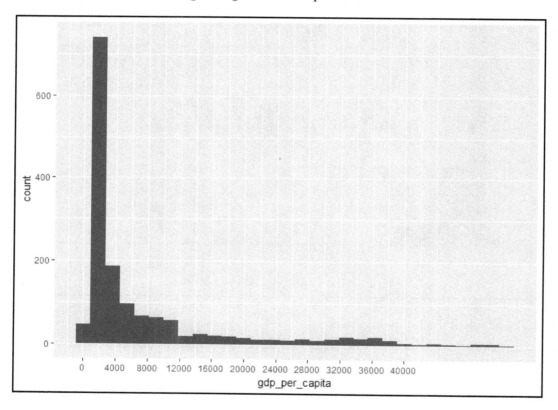

The answer to the last question is as follows: the maximum GDP per capita is about 2,000. This is a left-skewed histogram.

Types of Coordinates

Let's explore the types of coordinates:

- **Cartesian** (`coord_cartesian()`): ggplot uses a Cartesian coordinate system by default, but sometimes, one might want to use polar coordinates, which is another way of looking at fractions. One possible use of the command is to transform a bar chart into a pie chart.
- **Polar** (`coord_polar()`): In ggplot2, the Cartesian coordinates (x, y) become the polar coordinates *theta* and *r*. You can specify which coordinate is *theta* and which is *r*.

Let's see an example to understand polar coordinates in the next section.

Understanding Polar Coordinates

In this section, we'll generate some numbers and plot them as Cartesian and polar coordinates.

Let's begin by implementing the following steps:

1. Generate angles between 0-360, in intervals of 15:

   ```
   t <- seq(0, 360, by=15).
   ```

2. Define another variable - the radius `r`:

   ```
   r <- 2.
   ```

3. Use qplot to plot the vectors in Cartesian coordinates (`Plot1`). What do you see? Write your answer as a comment in the code:

   ```
   qplot(r,t)
   ```

    Your first plot should look like plot 1.

4. Use qplot to plot the vectors in polar coordinates. What do you see? Write your answer:

   ```
   qplot(r,t)+coord_polar(theta="y").
   ```

5. Use **scales** to change the labeling and make it look like plot 3. Here, we define the range from 0-360, with breaks of 30:

```
qplot(r,t)+coord_polar(theta="y")+scale_y_continuous(breaks=seq(0,3
60,30)).
```

Refer to the complete code at `https://goo.gl/RheL2G`.

Plot 1 is as follows:

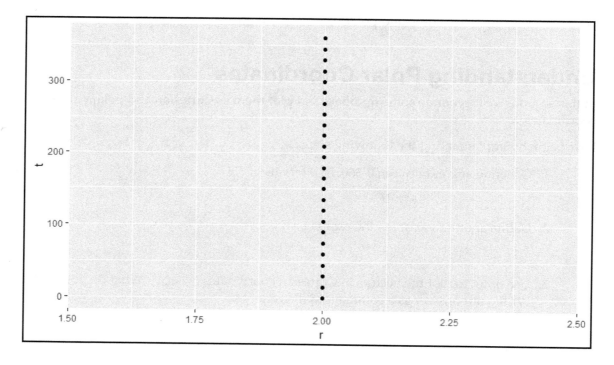

Plot 2 is as follows:

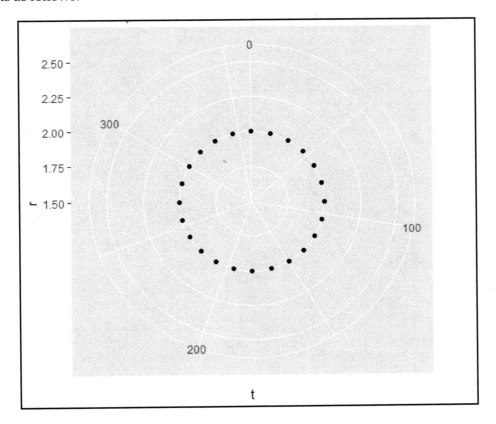

The final plot is as follows:

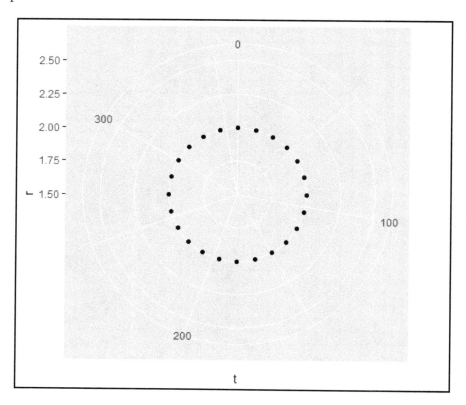

Various label formats are available, and you can change label formats as well. The following label formats are available:

- `scales::comma_format()` adds commas, in order to make it easier to read large numbers.
- `scales::unit_format(unit, scale)` adds a unit suffix and optionally, scaling.
- `scales::dollar_format(prefix, suffix)` displays currency values, rounding to two decimal places and adding a prefix or suffix.
- `scales::wrap_format()` wraps long labels into multiple lines.

We will combine all of the preceding commands to make a single plot.

Activity: Applying the Grammar of Graphics to Create a Complex Visualization

Scenario

Sometimes, you may need to customize a plot, changing scales and coordinate types. For example, you may have profits in billions (or trillions) of dollars, and wish to represent a big number as 1M, 2M, and so on. Or, you may want to view percentages of profits per month as a pie chart. In such cases, you would need to change your Cartesian coordinates to polar coordinates.

Aim

To use the Grammar of Graphics to create a visualization.

Steps for Completion

1. Create the scatter plot using the ggplot commands.
2. Use the required dataset.
3. Change scales with one of the preceding label formats.

 Refer to the complete code at `https://goo.gl/RheL2G`.

The outcome will be a scatter plot that matches the following plot:

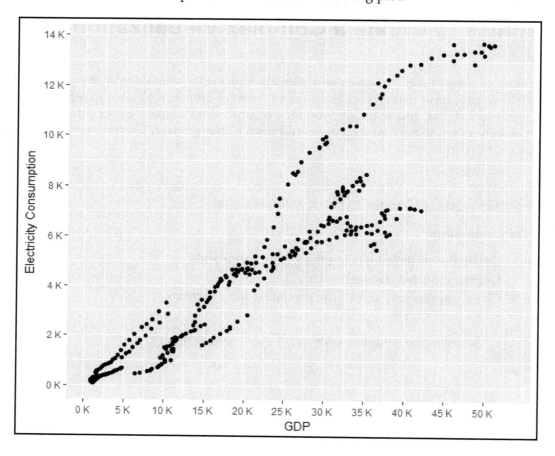

Facets

In data visualization, we sometimes have the need to compare different groups, looking at data alongside each other. One method for doing this is creating a subplot for each group. These kinds of plots are known as Trellis displays. In ggplot2, they're called facets. Facets divide the data by some discrete or categorical variable and display the same type of graph for each data subset.

Let's look at electricity consumption versus GDP for different countries, which we calculated in the previous activity.

We don't know which country has the highest GDP or electricity consumption. Let's split the data now.

Using Facets to Split Data

In this section, we'll plot subsets of data as separate subplots. Let's begin by implementing the following steps:

1. Use the `gapminder.csv` dataset.
2. Make a scatter plot of `Electricity_consumption_per_capita` versus `gdp_per_capita`:

   ```
   p <- ggplot (df, aes (x=gdp_per_capita,
   y=Electricity_consumption_per_capita)) + geom_point ()
   ```

3. Use `facet_grid()` to specify the variables to split upon. We will need to plot the electricity consumption versus GDP separately for each country. So, our split variable will be `Country`:

   ```
   p + facet_grid(Country ~ .)
   ```

Take a look at the following output scatter plot:

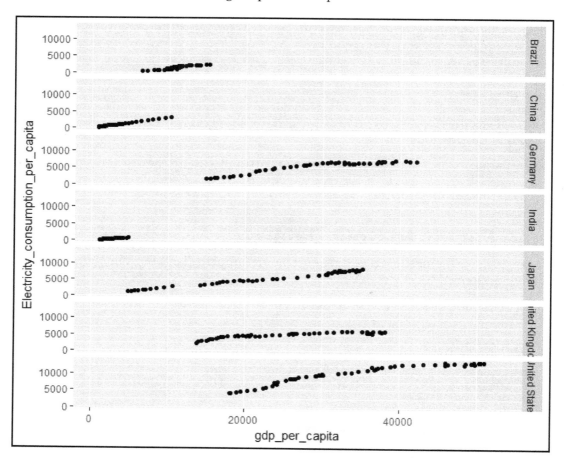

4. You can also arrange the panels vertically:

```
p + facet_grid(. ~ Country)):
```

Take a look at the following output scatter plot:

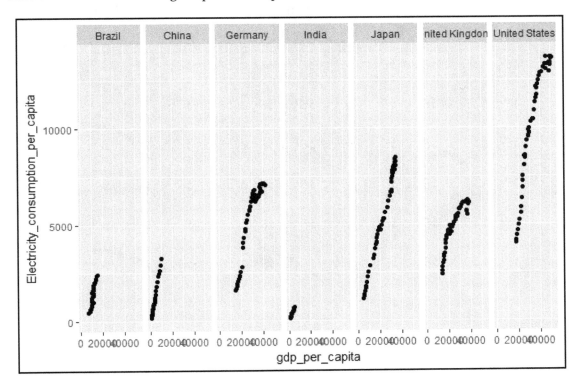

 Refer to the complete code at: `https://goo.gl/RheL2G`.

Another command that can be used is `facet_wrap()`. With the `facet_wrap()` command, the subplots are laid out horizontally, and then wrapped around like words on a page. A `facet_wrap()` plot would look as follows:

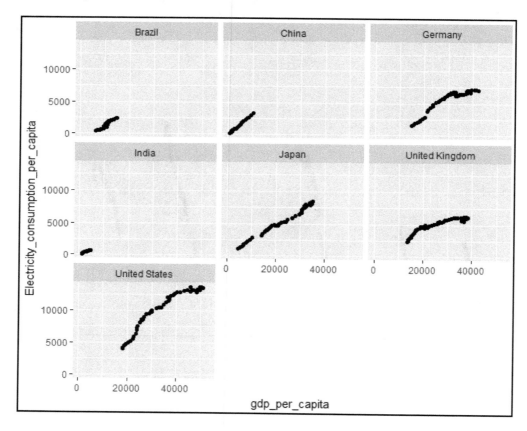

Activity: Using Faceting to Understand Data

Scenario

Here you want to look at the distribution of loan amounts for different credit grades.

Aim

To plot the loan amount for different credit grades using faceting.

Steps for Completion

1. Use the loan data and plot a histogram.
2. Use the required command to plot the loan data.
3. Change the default options for `facet_wrap`.

Outcome

Take a look at the following outcome plots, plot 1:

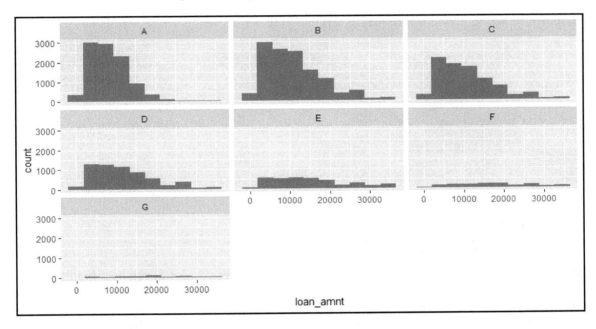

Plot 2:

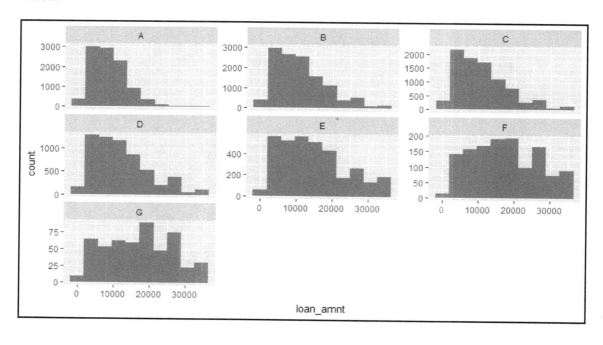

Changing Styles and Colors

Aside from faceting, we can also produce a color differentiated plot. It can be advantageous to use a color differentiated plot when the shapes are very similar and there is some overlap. To see small differences, it is useful to use colors. For example, we can plot the Electricity consumption versus GDP by using different colors or shapes for the countries.

Using Different Colors to Group Points by a Variable

In this section, we'll produce a color differentiated scatter plot with respect to a third variable. Let's begin by implementing the following steps:

1. Choose a subset of dataset 1 (`gapminder`) and select a few countries. Use the following subset command:

   ```
   dfs <- subset(df,Country %in%c("Germany","India","China","United
   States"))
   ```

2. Make a scatter plot of the two variables and change the x and y titles:

   ```
   p1<-
   ggplot(df,aes_string(x=var1,y=var2))+)geom_point(color=2,shape=2)+x
   lim(0,10000)+xlab(name1)+ylab(name2)
   ```

3. Then, change the colors and shapes of the points for plot 1:

   ```
   p2 <-
   ggplot(df,aes_string(x=var1,y=var2))+geom_t(aes(color=Country,shape
   =Country))+xlim(0,10000)+xlab(name1)+ylab(name2)
   ```

4. Now, group points by `Country`, mapped by color and shape, for plot 3 and plot 4:

   ```
   grid.arrange(p1, p2, nrow = 2)
   ```

Refer to the complete code at `https://goo.gl/RheL2G`.

The following plots should be obtained on completion of this example:

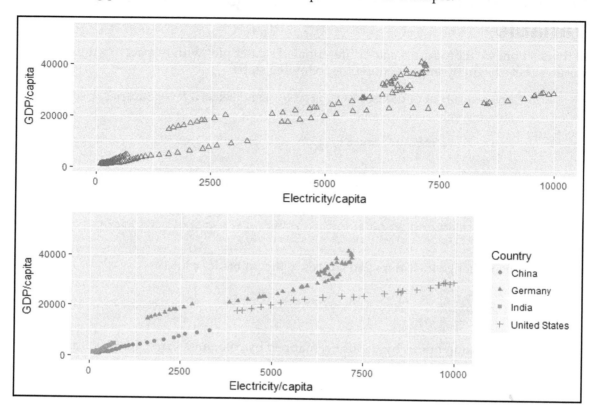

Activity: Using Color Differentiation in Plots

Scenario

Suppose that a loan company has given loans to people with different features (for example, employment status, home ownership, credit grade, and so on), and you want to see the relationships between some of those variables.

Aim

To view the distribution of loan amount versus home ownership using a plot with color differentiation on the basis of credit grade.

Steps for Completion

1. Use the `LoanStats` dataset and make a subset.
2. Clean the dataset (removing the `NONE` and `NA` cases).
3. Create a boxplot showing the loan amount versus home ownership.
4. Color differentiate by credit grade.

The following plot should be obtained:

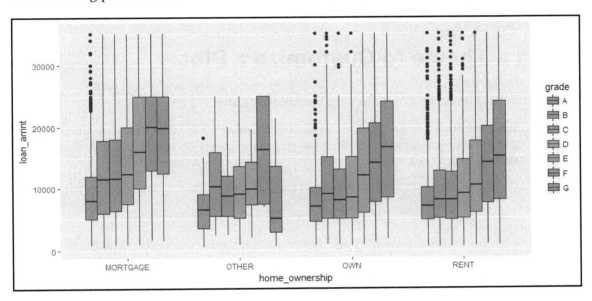

Themes and Changing the Appearance of Graphs

The Grammar of Graphics principle that underlies ggplot2 concerns how data is processed and displayed; it doesn't concern things such as fonts, background colors, and so on. To tune the appearances of these elements, ggplot2's theming system provides control over the appearance of non-data elements. In this book, we will touch upon a few thematic aspects. It will not be possible to go over all of the thematic options. For a more complete list of options, access the help guide by typing `?theme`, or look at the ggplot2 manual.

Themes can be changed in multiple ways, as follows:

- Changing them individually for each plot
- Using a predefined theme
- Defining your own theme and using it for all of your plots

The following example is intended to introduce you to the elements of different themes. The plot that we will produce at the end is not necessarily the best visual choice; it is primarily created to illustrate the options.

Using a Theme to Customize a Plot

In this example, we'll use thematic commands to customize and improve a plot's appearance. Let's begin by implementing the following steps:

1. Let's use the `HollywoodMovies` data and create a bar chart of movie titles and their world gross amounts. Since we have too many objects, we will make a subset, as follows:

```
dfn <- subset (HollywoodMovies, Genre
%in%c("Action","Adventure","Comedy","Drama","Romance") & LeadStudio
%in%c("Fox","Sony","Columbia","Paramount","Disney")).
```

2. Let's predefine a theme. Type ?theme (alternatively, when you type theme, R shows you the options available; see the screenshots that follow). Some of the available options are as follows:

Arguments	
line	all line elements (element_line)
rect	all rectangular elements (element_rect)
text	all text elements (element_text)
title	all title elements: plot, axes, legends (element_text; inherits from text)
aspect.ratio	aspect ratio of the panel
axis.title	label of axes (element_text; inherits from text)
axis.title.x	x axis label (element_text; inherits from axis.title)
axis.title.x.top	x axis label on top axis (element_text; inherits from axis.title.x)
axis.title.y	y axis label (element_text; inherits from axis.title)
axis.title.y.right	y axis label on right axis (element_text; inherits from axis.title.y)
axis.text	tick labels along axes (element_text; inherits from text)

3. Note that `axis.title` is of the type `element_text`, which inherits from `text`.

4. We will therefore change aspects of `element_text`. Type `? element_text` to bring up the options. Use the following table to change some of the thematic aspects:

Argument	Type	Values
axis.title.x	Element_ text	size=15, family="Helvetica", angle=45
axis.title.y	Element_ text	size=15, family="Helvetica", angle=45
Panel.grid. major	Element_ line	color="gray87"
Panel. background	Element_ rect	Fill="Beige"
plot. background	Element_ rect	Fill="Gray",size=20

R will autofill and display the options before you finish typing, as shown in the following screenshot:

```
◇ theme                {ggplot2}  ^   theme(line, rect, text, title, aspect.ratio,
◈ theme_bw             {ggplot2}         axis.title, axis.title.x, axis.title.x.top,
◈ theme_classic        {ggplot2}         axis.title.y, axis.title.y.right, axis.text,
◈ theme_dark           {ggplot2}         axis.text.x, axis.text.x.top, axis.text.y,
◈ theme_get            {ggplot2}         axis.text.y.right, axis.ticks, axis.ticks.x,
◈ theme_gray           {ggplot2}         axis.ticks.y, axis.ticks.length, axis.line,
◈ theme_grey           {ggplot2}         axis.line.x, axis.line.y, legend.background,
◈ theme_light          {ggplot2}  v      legend.margin, legend.spacing, legend.spacing.x,
                                         legend.spacing.y, legend.key, legend.key.size,
                                         legend.key.height, legend.key.width, legend.text,
                                         legend.text.align, legend.title,
                                   Press F1 for additional help
```

Setting the `axis.title` options will bring up the following options for `element_text`:

```
> p2 <- p1+geom_bar(stat="identity",aes(fill=Lead;
> p3 <- p2+theme(axis.title.x=element_text(size=1
+     axis.title.y=element_text(size=15),
+     plot.background=element_rect(fill="Gray")
+     )
> p3
Warning message:
Removed 3 rows containing missing values (geom_bar
> p2
Warning message:
Removed 3 rows contai       element_text
> theme(axis.title.x=element_te
```

```
element_text(family = NULL, face = NULL, colour =
  NULL, size = NULL, hjust = NULL, vjust = NULL,
  angle = NULL, lineheight = NULL, color = NULL,
  margin = NULL, debug = NULL, inherit.blank =
  FALSE)
```

In conjunction with the theme system, the element_ functions specify the display of how non-data components of the plot are a drawn.

- element_blank: draws nothing, and assigns no space.

Press F1 for additional help

6. After studying the preceding options, define a theme to produce the following plot (also, see the code):

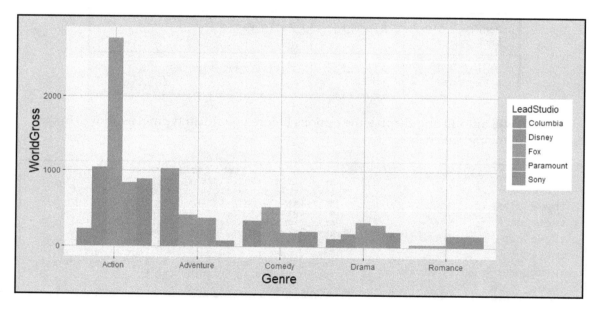

 The complete code is pasted here: `https://goo.gl/RheL2G`.

Analysis

The preceding plot shows the **World Gross amount** for the different genres, colored according to the different production houses. As you can see, the **Action** genre has the maximum earnings, and most of the movies are produced by **Fox**. **Disney** also earns more than other houses. **Disney** earns more than **Fox** for the **Adventure** genre.

You now have the tools to customize and improve this plot.

Using a predefined theme: There are some predefined themes that can be used. The same plots produced using different themes are shown here:

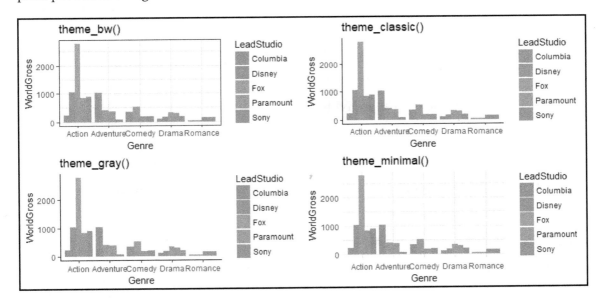

The color palette can be found at: `http://www.stat.columbia.edu/~tzheng/files/Rcolor.pdf`.

Using or Setting Your Own Theme Globally

In this section, we'll set our own theme for an individual (or global) plot. Let's begin by implementing the following steps:

1. Set up your theme, as follows:
   - Change the legend title and position.
   - Change the axes titles' colors and relative size (1.5). Using text changes the colors of the axes titles and the legend text, but not the label text.
   - Change the axes labels' text sizes; use axis.text: (Note that if you want to change the x and y axes separately, you should use axis.text.x and axis.text.y.)

   ```
   mytheme <- theme(text = element_text(color="Blue"),
   axis.text = element_text(size=12),axis.title =
   element_text(size = rel(1.5)))
   ```

2. Use your theme with an individual plot:

   ```
   p2 <- p1+mytheme
   ```

   (Click on **zoom plot** if it's not clear or is compressed in the canvas.)

3. You can also set it globally for all plots at the beginning of your code:

   ```
   (theme_set(mytheme)).
   ```

The plots with our theme are as follows:

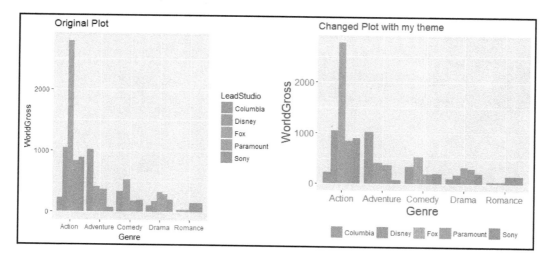

The default colors aren't always the most appealing; you may therefore want to use a different palette, by using the commands `scale_colour_brewer ()`, `scale_fill_brewer`, or `scale_colour_manual()`.

 Refer to the complete code here: `https://goo.gl/RheL2G`.

Changing the Color Scheme of the Given Theme

In this section, we'll change the color scheme and use a different palette. Let's begin by implementing the following steps:

1. Use the predefined theme, `theme_bw`, and create the same plot as in the previous example:

   ```
   (p2+theme_bw()+ggtitle("theme_bw()"))
   ```

   Now, we will use a different color palette.

2. The `?scale_fill_brewer` command provides the following palettes (the code snippets are included):

   Palettes

   The following palettes are available for use with these scales:

   Diverging

       BrBG, PiYG, PRGn, PuOr, RdBu, RdGy, RdYlBu, RdYlGn, Spectral

   Qualitative

       Accent, Dark2, Paired, Pastel1, Pastel2, Set1, Set2, Set3

   Sequential

       Blues, BuGn, BuPu, GnBu, Greens, Greys, Oranges, OrRd, PuBu, PuBuGn, PuRd, Purples, RdPu, Reds, YlGn, YlGnBu, YlOrBr, YlOrRd

   ---

3. Try using `Spectral`, `Pastel1`, and `Oranges` to produce the following plots:

   ```
   p4 + scale_fill_brewer(palette="Spectral")
   ```

Let's take a look at plot 1:

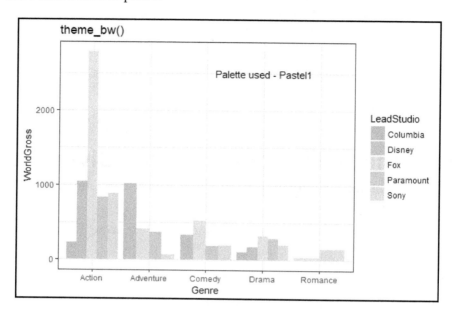

Let's take a look at plot 2:

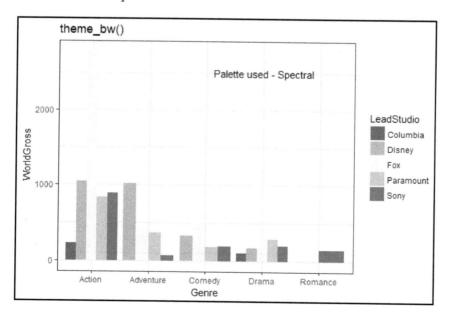

Let's take a look at plot 3:

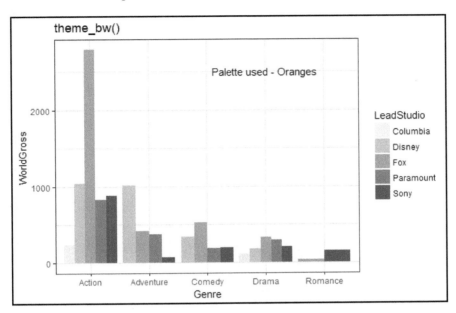

Activity: Using Themes and Color Differentiation in a Plot

Scenario

The need to compare two variables and differentiate by color may arise in certain cases; for example, a digital marketing company might wish to compare the number of views of its ad on different websites, or to compare the number of clicks versus the number of views for different states on the same website.

Aim

To plot the BMIs of males versus females in different countries and analyze the plot.

Steps for Completion

1. Make a scatter plot of female versus male BMIs.
2. Building your plot in layers, to avoid creating three separate plots.

The following plots will be obtained, plot 1:

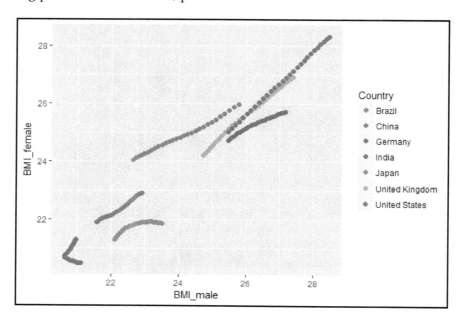

Plot 2:

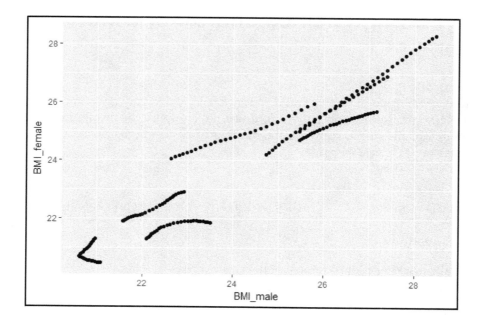

Plot 3:

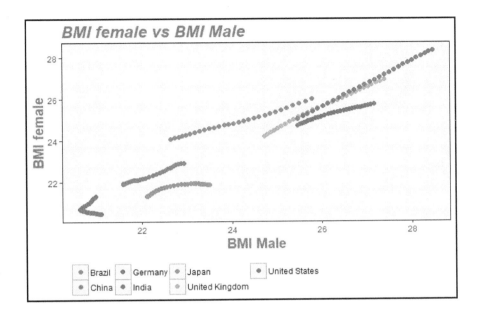

Geoms and Statistical Summaries

Sometimes, you will need to calculate statistical summaries, such as the mean, median, or a quartile of a variable, and view changes with respect to another variable. This can be done by using **grouping** commands.

Let's plot `Genre` versus `AudienceScore` for the `HollywoodMovies` dataset.
Change the angle of the axis labeling text, in order to make it less cluttered, using the following command:

```
ggplot(HollywoodMovies,aes(Genre,AudienceScore))+geom_point()+theme
(axis.text.x=element_text(angle=40))
```

You'll get the following output:

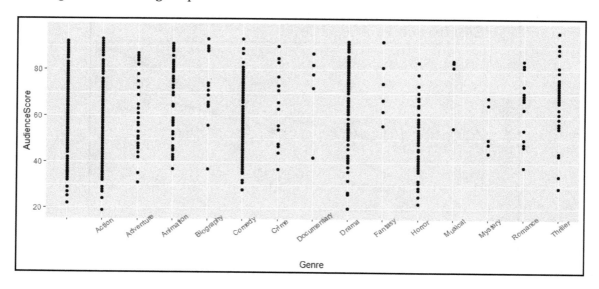

Using Grouping to Create a Summarized Plot

In this section, we'll use grouping to summarize multiple *y* values for a given *x* value. Let's begin by implementing the following steps:

1. Use grouping to group by genre and remove NULL values:

    ```
    gp_scr <- group_by(HollywoodMovies,Genre)
    gp_scr <- na.omit(gp_scr)
    ```

2. Calculate the mean and standard deviation using the summarise function and make a new dataset, as follows:

    ```
    dfnew <-
    dplyr::summarise(gp_scr,as_mean=mean(AudienceScore),as_sd=sd(Audien
    ceScore),n=n())
    ```

3. We want to make a plot with scores ordered by means. Follow the steps in the code to do so. Plot the means, as follows:

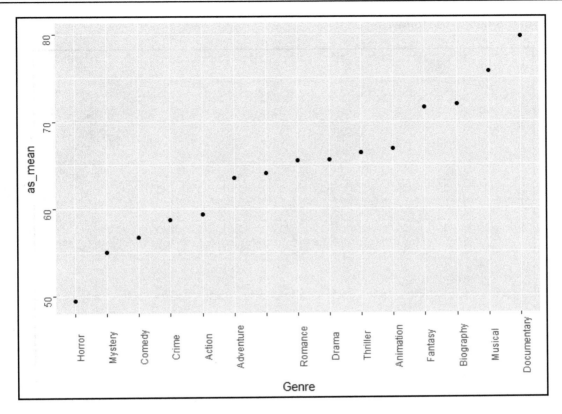

4. Make the final plot, adding error bars, as follows:

```
ggplot(data = dfnew,
aes(x=Genre,y=as_mean))+geom_errorbar(color="red",aes(ymin=as_mean-
(as_sd/sqrt(n-1)), ymax =
as_mean+(as_sd/sqrt(n-1))))+ylab("Audiencescore
Mean")+theme(axis.text = element_text(angle=90))
```

Refer to the complete code here: https://goo.gl/RheL2G.

You should obtain the following plot:

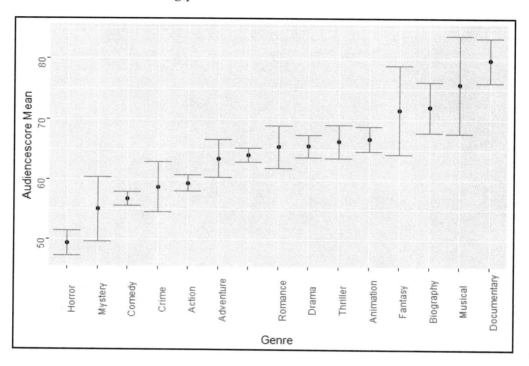

Summary

In this chapter, you learned about the Grammar of Graphics in detail, changing the various theme and color aspects of graphs to create better visuals and reveal further details about data. You also learned how to provide more useful information in scatter plots, using grouping and summarizing to calculate quantities such as the mean, median, quartile, and so on.

In the next chapter, we will work on more advanced plotting techniques, which are not needed quite as often but may be required in some cases.

Advanced Geoms and Statistics

3

In this chapter, we will learn how to create some specialized graphs. When we have data that is correlated, we may need to depict multiple variables in one plot. We will work on some advanced plotting techniques that combine information from three or more variables in one graph, understand how to view data that varies with time, depict geographically dependent data separately into different regions of a map, and gain an understanding of trends and correlations between variables and different ways to view them.

By the end of this chapter, you will be able to:

- Create various types of plots using advanced plotting techniques
- Create and superimpose density plots for comparing distributions
- Construct time series plots and color differentiated maps
- Utilize trends, correlations, and statistical summaries to reveal data insights

Advanced Plotting Techniques

Two of the most common advanced plotting techniques are scatter plots and bubble charts. **Scatter plots** show the relationship between two variables. A **bubble chart** can include a third variable. Each point (with its values (v1, v2, v3) of associated data) is plotted as a disk, where two of the values show the x and y locations, and the third depicts the size. Just like in a scatter plot, a bubble chart uses numerical variables for its x and y axes. You cannot use categorical variables in a bubble chart.

In this plot, we will plot the electricity consumption per capita for different years and different countries. The size of the point will vary, according to the population of the country.

Creating a Bubble Chart

In this section, we'll create a bubble chart showing the relationship between electricity consumption in different years for different countries. Let's begin by implementing the following steps:

1. Make a subset of the dataset.
2. Use `geom_point` to make a scatter plot.
3. Specify the color as the country and the size as the population in the aesthetics.
4. Set the limits by using the `coord_cartesian` command.
5. Set the labels for the *y*-axis and the title.
6. Set the theme as the classic theme.

 You can read more about the specifications at: `http://ggplot2.tidyverse.org/articles/ggplot2-specs.html`.

Run the following code to create the bubble chart:

```
dfs <- subset(df,Country %in% c("Germany","India","China","United
States","Japan"))
ggplot(dfs,aes(x=Year,y=Electricity_consumption_per_capita)) +
geom_point(aes(size=population,color=Country))+
coord_cartesian(xlim=c(1950,2020))+labs(subtitle="Electricity consumption
vs Year",title="Bubble chart")+ylab("Electricity
consumption")+scale_size(breaks=c(0,1e+8,0.3e+9,0.5e+9,1e+9,1.5e+9),range=c
(1,5))
```

Take a look at the following output screenshot:

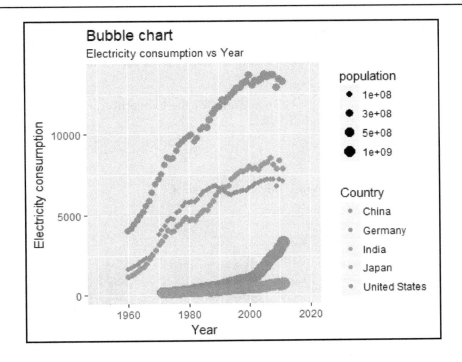

Density Plots

When the statistics are low, histograms are ineffective at determining the shape of a distribution, because they are so strongly affected by the number of bins used.

A density plot is an alternative, in order to see the distribution of the data. It uses an estimation technique to convert the histogram into a continuous curve and plot the probability distribution of the data. The area of a density plot is usually scaled to unity.

Sometimes, you might need to compare two histograms with different amounts of data, while also wanting to see the shapes of the histograms. For example, you might wish to compare the age distribution of clients from a bigger and a smaller company that sell similar products. You would like to overlay the two histograms, but since the smaller company has very few clients, it is difficult to compare the two. In such cases, instead of plotting the total amount of data, you can plot the probability density.

Using Density Plots

In this section, we'll use density plots to compare loan distributions for different credit grades.

1. Use the loan data and plot a histogram for the loan amounts. Subdivide it into the different grades, as follows:

```
ggplot(df3,aes(x=loan_amnt)) + geom_histogram() + facet_
wrap(~grade)
```

Take a look at the following output screenshot:

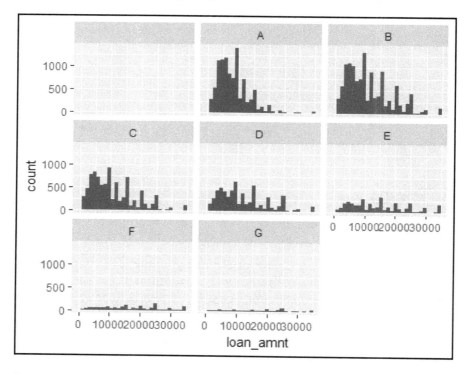

2. We cannot see the shapes of the **E**, **F**, and **G** grades very clearly. Also, all of the grades have different histogram counts. Let's use a density plot to compare them, as follows:

```
ggplot(df3,aes(x=loan_amnt)) + geom_density() + facet_wrap(~grade)
```

Take a look at the following output screenshot:

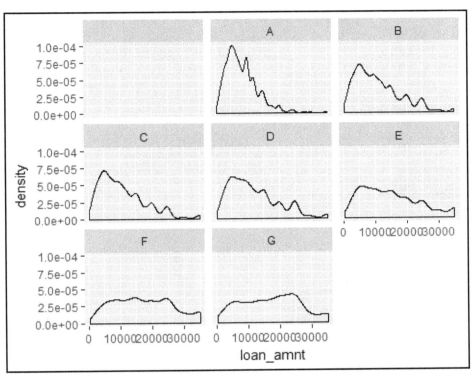

Analysis

Density plots make it much easier to see the shapes. All of the plots are normalized to unit area, which means adjusting the values measured on different scales to a common scale. You can see that for the **F** and **G** grades, the loan amounts are much broader, and almost all of the loan amounts have equal probabilities, but for **A**, **B**, **C**, and **D**, you can see right-skewed histograms, implying that most people in these credit grades take out smaller loans, of about 5,000. The distribution for credit grade **A** is narrowest, and the distribution becomes broader as the credit grade worsens.

 You can read more about the specs at:
`http://serialmentor.com/dataviz/histograms-density-plots.html`

Superimposing Plots

Sometimes, it's easier to compare shapes when we superimpose plots. In the previous example, we created density plots, using `facet_wrap` to subdivide the data into different credit grades. We can also superimpose plots and use different fill colors to differentiate between them. Consider the following code:

```
ggplot(df3,aes(x=loan_amnt)) + geom_density(aes(fill=grade),alpha=1/2) +
scale_fill_brewer(palette="Dark2") + xlab("Loan Amount") + theme_light()
```

Here, our geom object is `geom_density`. The alpha parameter sets the transparency level (we set it to 50%). We chose a customized palette for the fill colors, using the `scale_fill_brewer` command. Take a look at the following output screenshot:

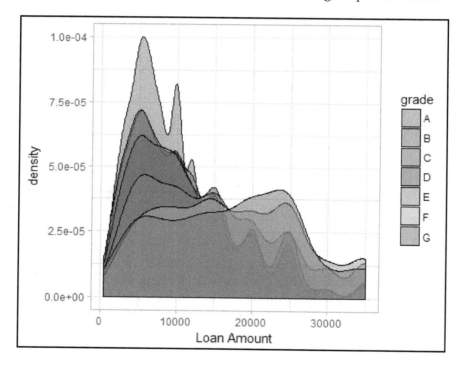

Using Density Plots to Compare Distributions

Scenario

Comparing the distribution of sales for different car models in a car company.

Aim

To use density plots to compare distributions.

Steps for Completion

1. Use the dataset provided.
2. Compare the TIP amount for various days.
3. Superimpose all of the plots.
4. Use the required command for the x-axis tick marks.
5. Reproduce the plot that follows:

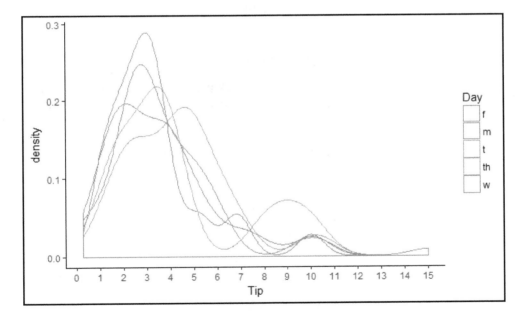

 Refer to the complete code at: https://goo.gl/x4wQHG.

Time Series

A time series is a sequence of data points that are recorded at specific times. Time series are often used in the fiance, trading, and housing industries. They are also used by scientists for predicting earthquakes, weather, and so on. Any data that has a certain pattern with regards to time (which could be days, weeks, months, or years) can be used to predict a future pattern (known as forecasting). In the trading industry, for example, it's useful to predict future stock prices. Please see the reference within the following note for more information on time series.

 You can read more about the specialty at: https://onlinecourses. science.psu.edu/stat510/node/47/.

To illustrate a time series plot, let's use the FB.csv dataset. It contains fiance data related to FB, and was downloaded from Yahoo Finance. See the references at the end of the example for information on how this data was downloaded.

Creating a Time Series Plot

In this section, we'll look at variations in closing stock prices for Facebook from June 2017 to June 2018. Let's begin by implementing the following steps:

1. Read the data provided in FB.csv.

2. Print the data using the glimpse command, as follows:

```
df_fb <- read.csv("data/FB.csv")
#Glimpse
glimpse(df_fb)
## Observations: 357
## Variables: 7
## $ Date <fct> 2017-01-17, 2017-01-18, 2017-01-19, 2017-01-20,
2017...
## $ Open <dbl> 128.04, 128.41, 128.23, 128.10, 127.31, 129.38,
130....
## $ High <dbl> 128.34, 128.43, 128.35, 128.48, 129.25, 129.90,
131....
## $ Low <dbl> 127.40, 126.84, 127.45, 126.78, 126.95, 128.38,
129....
## $ Close <dbl> 127.87, 127.92, 127.55, 127.04, 128.93, 129.37,
131....
## $ Adj.Close <dbl> 127.87, 127.92, 127.55, 127.04, 128.93,
```

```
129.37, 131....
## $ Volume <int> 15228000, 13145900, 12195500, 19097200, 16593600,
15...
```

 There are 21 observations, with variables such as the `Date` and the `Open` and `Close` prices. Let's plot the daily `Close` prices as a time series.

Run the following code to create the time series plot:

```
#Convert date to Character
df_fb$Date <- as.Date(df_fb$Date)
#Daily data plot
ggplot(df_fb,aes(x=Date,y=Close, group=1)) +
geom_line(color="black",na.rm=TRUE)+
ggtitle("Daily Closing Stock Prices: Facebook") + theme(plot.title =
element_text(lineheight=.7, face="bold")) + scale_x_date(date_breaks='3
month')+ theme_bw()
```

Take a look at the following output screenshot:

Explanation of the Code

When we use `geom_line`, we need to specify `group=1`, because for line graphs, the data points must be grouped. In this case, since all of the points should be connected, the value of the `group=1`. When more variables are used and multiple lines are drawn, the line grouping is usually done by a variable.

Now, instead of a time series depicting daily prices, we would like to make a plot of prices for every month and also look at the mean closing price for every month.

Activity: Plot the Monthly Closing Stock Prices and the Mean Values

Scenario

We are interested in looking at the monthly fluctuations in stock prices (as daily stock prices have too much variation) and identifying any trends.

Aim

To plot the monthly closing stock prices, and then use the summary tools to plot the mean closing stock price.

Steps for Completion

1. Use the `strftime` command to get the month from each date and make another variable (Month).
2. Change the month to a numerical value by using as.numeric.
3. Now, use ggplot to make a plot of closing prices versus months.
4. Plot the data using `geom_point (color=red)`.
5. Change the x scale to show each month, and label the x-axis, such that each month is shown.
6. Title your plot **Monthly closing stock prices: Facebook**.

The following is a screenshot of the output:

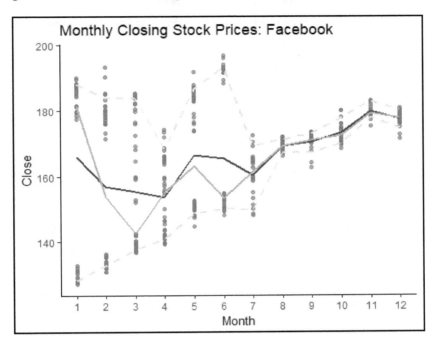

Analysis

As you can see, although the closing prices have a lot of fluctuation during each month, the mean has less variation and indicates some trends; we can conclude that the closing prices get slightly higher as we approach December.

Maps

Sometimes, we want to know the trends and behaviors of people in different countries or states. For example, we might want to see the shopping behaviors of people in different states. The maps package is useful for this purpose. In this section, we will look at how to draw and display information with maps.

Displaying Information with Maps

In this section, we'll create a map of the US and Europe that is colored according to `lat`, `long`, and `group` variables. Let's begin by implementing the following steps:

1. Install the `maps` package using `map_data` to get a data frame for the different states' information, as follows:

```
states_map <- map_data("state")
glimpse(states_map)
## Observations: 15,537
## Variables: 6
## $ long <dbl> -87.46201, -87.48493, -87.52503, -87.53076,
-87.5708...
## $ lat <dbl> 30.38968, 30.37249, 30.37249, 30.33239, 30.32665,
30...
## $ group <dbl> 1, 1, 1, 1, 1, 1, 1, 1, 1, 1, 1, 1, 1, 1, 1, 1, 1,
1...
## $ order <int> 1, 2, 3, 4, 5, 6, 7, 8, 9, 10, 11, 12, 13, 14, 15,
1...
## $ region <chr> "alabama", "alabama", "alabama", "alabama",
"alabama...
## $ subregion <chr> NA, NA, NA, NA, NA, NA, NA, NA, NA, NA, NA,
NA, NA, ...
```

The `map_data()` function returns a data frame with the following columns:

`long`: Longitude.

`lat`: Latitude.

`group`: This is a grouping variable for each polygon.

A region or subregion can have multiple polygons (for example, if it includes islands).

Now, we can plot the data using `geom_polygon()` (which can include a color fill) or `geom_path()` (which cannot include a color fill). By default, the latitude and longitude will be drawn on a Cartesian coordinate plane, but you can also use `coord_map()` to specify a projection. The default projection is `mercator`, which unlike the Cartesian plane, has progressively changing spacing of the grid lines for the latitude lines.

2. Run the following code to obtain the maps:

```
ggplot(states_map, aes(x=long, y=lat, group=group)) +
geom_polygon(fill="white", colour="black")
ggplot(states_map, aes(x=long, y=lat, group=group)) + geom_path() +
coord_map("mercator")
```

Take a look at the following output screenshots, output 1:

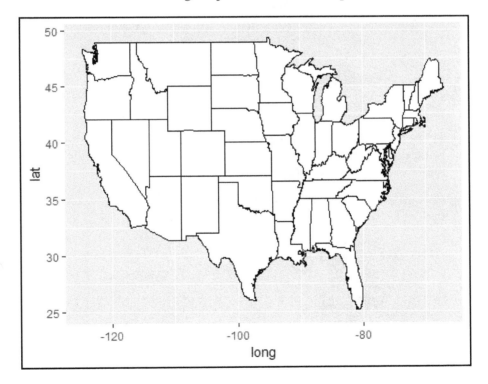

Output 2:

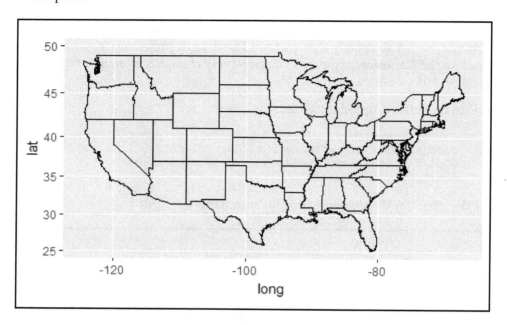

 There are a number of different maps available, including the world, France, Italy, the USA (an outline of the United States), states (each state in the USA), and counties (each county in the USA).

3. For example, we can get the map data for the world, but draw only certain regions, as follows:

```
#Get map data for world
world_map <- map_data("world")
europe <- map_data("world", region=c("Germany", "Spain", "Italy",
"France","UK","Ireland"))
ggplot(europe, aes(x=long, y=lat, group=group, fill=region)) +
geom_polygon(colour="black") + scale_fill_ brewer(palette="Set3")
```

Take a look at the following output screenshot:

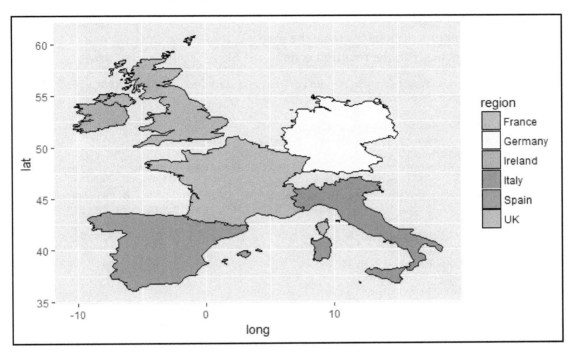

Activity: Creating a Variable-Encoded Regional Map

Scenario

A company wants to know which states buy their product the most. A colored map is a clear way of showing this information. Here, we use the data to create a map, differentiated with the percentage of voters that voted for Obama.

Aim

To create a map of the US that is colored according to the percentage of voters that voted for Obama.

Steps for Completion

1. Merge the data sets.
2. Use the ggplot options to create the map.
3. For aesthetics, run the required code:

```
USStates$Statelower <- as.character(tolower(USStates$State))
glimpse(USStates)
## Observations: 50
## Variables: 23
## $ State <fct> Alabama, Alaska, Arizona,
Arkansas, Californi...
## $ HouseholdIncome <dbl> 43.253, 70.760, 49.774, 40.768, 61.094,
58.43...
## $ Region <fct> S, W, W, S, W, W, NE, NE, S, S, W, W, MW, MW,...
## $ Population <dbl> 4.849, 0.737, 6.731, 2.966, 38.803, 5.356,
3....
## $ EighthGradeMath <dbl> 269.2, 281.6, 279.7, 277.9, 275.9,
289.7, 285...
## $ HighSchool <dbl> 84.9, 92.8, 85.6, 87.1, 84.1, 89.5, 91.0,
86....
## $ College <dbl> 24.9, 24.7, 25.5, 22.4, 31.4, 37.0, 39.8, 31....
## $ IQ <dbl> 95.7, 99.0, 97.4, 97.5, 95.5, 101.6, 103.1, 1...
## $ GSP <dbl> 32.615, 61.156, 35.195, 31.837, 46.029, 46.24...
## $ Vegetables <dbl> 74.2, 80.8, 76.2, 72.0, 82.7, 80.9, 77.8,
71....
## $ Fruit <dbl> 54.1, 60.3, 60.5, 49.5, 69.6, 64.3, 66.3, 59....
## ggplot(us_data, aes(x=long, y=lat, group=group, fill=ObamaVote))
+ geom_polygon(colour="black") +
coord_map("mercator")+scale_fill_gradient(low="red",high="blue")
```

Take a look at the following output screenshot:

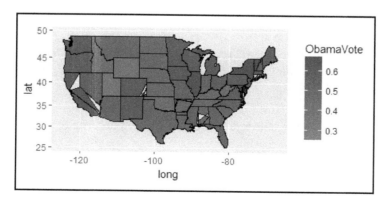

Electoral college
maps: https://www.nytimes.com/2016/08/23/upshot/50-years-of-elec
toral-college-maps-how-the-us-turned-red-and-blue.html.

Trends, Correlations, and Statistical Summaries

Statistical summaries are useful for summarizing a group of points. You may want to see different quantities (such as the minimum, maximum, mean, median, or quantiles) for a time series plot or a line chart that includes multiple y values for a given x value. We will use the financial data from Facebook and the statistical summary tool to better understand the trends.

Creating a Time Series Plot with the Mean, Median, and Quantiles

In this section, we'll create a time series plot, and then plot its mean, median, and 10% and 90% quantiles. Let's execute the following code:

```
ggplot(df_fb, aes(Month,Close)) + geom_point(color="red",alpha=1/2,position
= position_
jitter(h=0.0,w=0.0))+ geom_line(stat='summary',fun.y=mean,
color="blue",size=1)+geom_line(stat='summary',fun.y=median,
color="orange",size=1)+geom_line(stat='summary',fun.y=quantile, fun.
args=list(probs=0.1),
linetype=2,color='green',size=1.)+geom_line(stat='summary',fun.y=quantile,
fun.
args=list(probs=0.9),linetype=2,color='green',size=1.)+scale_x_continuous(b
reaks=seq(0,13,1))+
ggtitle("Monthly Closing Stock Prices: Facebook")+theme_classic()
```

Take a look at the following output screenshot:

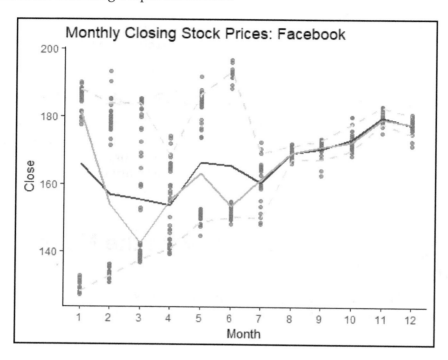

Analysis

The mean is shown in blue, while the median is shown in orange. The 10% and 90% quantiles are the dotted green lines.

Trends, Correlations, and Scatter plots

You can study trends in data by looking at scatter plots of two variables. This can reveal whether one variable is related to another variable. If variable A increases as variable B increases, it is considered a positive correlation. If variable A decreases as variable B increases, it is considered a negative correlation. If there is no clear trend, then it is considered a zero correlation. The values of the correlation coefficient can be from -1 to +1.

To study whether there is a trend, you can add a trend line by fitting the points and studying the **goodness of fit**.

For example, we can add a linear regression line to a scatter plot. To do so, we will add `stat_smooth()` and tell it to use `method=lm`. This instructs it to fit the data with the `lm()` (linear model) function. Let's do this for the **gapminder** data.

Creating a Scatter Plot and Fitting a Linear Regression Model

To draw a scatter plot of the electricity consumption per capita against the GDP per capita, and then fit a regression model. Let's begin by implementing the following steps:

1. Use ggplot and specify the *x* and *y* aesthetics, as follows:

   ```
   X=gdp_per_capita, Y=Electricity_consumption_per_capita
   ```

2. Make a scatter plot using `geom_point`. The points should be color differentiated by `country (aes(color=Country) )`.
3. Set the appropriate x-axis limits (from 0-3,000).
4. Add a linear regression model, `stat_smooth (method=lm)`.

The points indicate a positive trend, which is also confirmed by the fitted line. In other words, electricity consumption is positively correlated to the GDP of a country:

```
ggplot(dfs,
aes(gdp_per_capita,Electricity_consumption_per_capita)) +
geom_point(aes(color=Country))+xlim(0,30000)+
stat_smooth(method=lm)
```

The plot will look as follows:

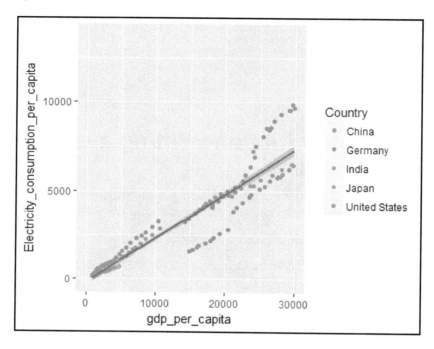

5. However, we would like to fit the points separately for each country. To do so, we must add the Country aesthetic to ggplot itself, as follows:

```
ggplot(dfs,
aes(gdp_per_capita,Electricity_consumption_per_capita,color=Country
)) + geom_point() + stat_smooth(method=lm)
```

The plot will look as follows:

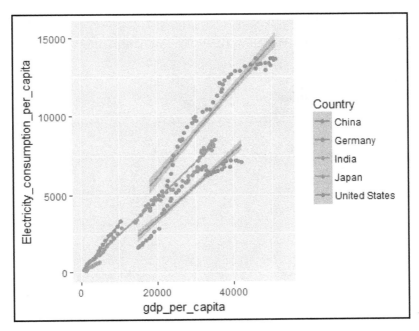

Before making individual scatter plots, we can also study the correlation of all of the variables by using a correlation plot. Install the `corrplot` package, and load it using `require(corrplot)`.

Creating a Correlation Plot

In this section, we'll make a correlation plot for all continuous variables in the `gapminder` dataset. Let's begin by implementing the following steps:

1. Choose only continuous variables by using the following command:

```
dfs1 <- dfs[,colnames(dfs)[4:9]]
```

2. Remove all NAs; otherwise, the correlation will not work, because it requires finite values:

```
dfs1 <- na.omit(dfs1)
```

3. Get the correlation matrix, M, using the following command:

```
M <- cor(dfs1)
```

4. Plot the correlation matrix using the following command:

```
corrplot(M,method="circle")
```

The plot will look as follows:

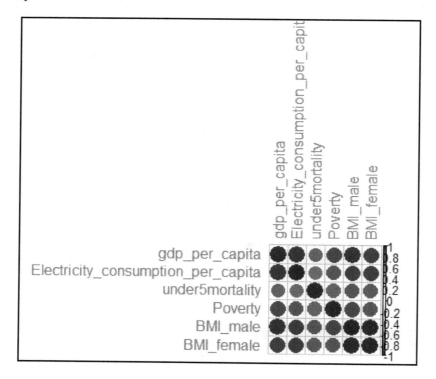

5. The preceding plot looks messy because of its long names. Let's change the long names to shorter names. Also, use another method for `corrplot("number")`, so that we can see the values of the correlation coefficients:

```
colnames(dfs1) <-
c("gdp","electricity","mort","pov","bmi_m","bmi_f")
M <- cor(dfs1) corrplot(M,method="number")
```

The plot will look as follows:

	gdp	electricity	mort	pov	bmi_m	bmi_f
gdp	1	0.95	-0.73	-0.86	0.97	0.92
electricity	0.95	1	-0.68	-0.8	0.93	0.93
mort	-0.73	-0.68	1	0.77	-0.79	-0.77
pov	-0.86	-0.8	0.77	1	-0.86	-0.79
bmi_m	0.97	0.93	-0.79	-0.86	1	0.98
bmi_f	0.92	0.93	-0.77	-0.79	0.98	1

You can also try other methods for the correlation plots, as follows:

```
corrplot(M,method="pie")
corrplot(M,method="ellipse")
```

The plot will look as follows:

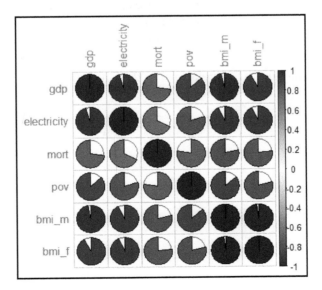

Analysis

In the first plot, the fractions in the pie give an idea of how strong the correlations are, and the colors indicate whether the correlations are positive or negative. In the second case, the width of the ellipse gives an indication of the correlation.

Activity: Studying Correlated Variables

Scenario

Sometimes, two variables are highly interdependent, and you'd like to study their variations in greater detail, and then fit a model to it. For example, Facebook might be interested in studying the correlation between the number of Facebook friends and the age of a user, to find out which age group utilizes Facebook the most. They might also be interested in finding out whether the variation is linear.

Aim

To make a scatter plot for the most correlated variables and then fit a linear regression model to it.

Steps for Completion

1. Make a subset of the `loan` dataset.
2. Use `cor` for the preceding loan data subset, and then choose two highly correlated variables in the loan dataset.
3. Make a scatter plot for the preceding pairs for grade A, then fit a linear regression model.
4. Determine what are the correlations of the preceding pairs.

Here are screenshots of the output plots:

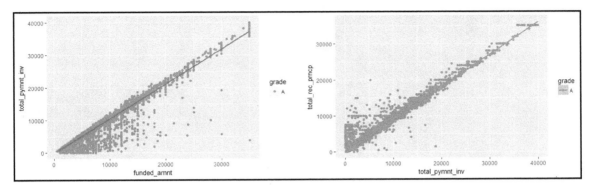

Analysis

Both of these plots reveal an (approximate) linear relationship between the preceding pairs, confirming the numbers that we obtained with the `cor` command.

Summary

In this chapter, we learned how to make some specialized graphs that may be needed in some specific scenarios, such as multiple variables, correlated variables, geographically varying data, and data varying with time.

Congratulations! We have completed the book on *Applied Data Visualization with R and ggplot2*. Continue to explore ggplot2 further, and use your skills to look at similar real-world problems, as covered in the course and in your work, and convert numbers into insightful, meaningful, and powerful visualizations.

Solutions

This section contains the worked-out answers for the activities present in each lesson. Note that in case of descriptive questions, your answers might not match the ones provided in this section completely. As long as the essence of the answers remain the same, you can consider them correct.

Chapter 1: Basic Plotting in ggplot2

The following are the activity solutions for this chapter.

Activity: Creating a Histogram and Explaining its Features

Steps for Completion:

1. Use the template code `Lesson1_student.R`.

 This is an empty code, wherein the libraries are already loaded. You will be writing your code here.

2. Load the dataset `temperature.csv` from the directory data.
3. Create the histogram for two cities (Vancouver and Miami) by using the command discussed previously.
4. Once the histogram is ready, run the code.
5. Analyze the two histograms by giving three points for each histogram, and two points of difference between the two.

Outcome:

Two histograms should be created and compared. The complete code is as follows:

```
df_t <- read.csv("data/historical-hourly-weather-data/temperature.
csv")
ggplot(df_t,aes(x=Vancouver))+geom_histogram()
ggplot(df_t,aes(x=Miami))+geom_histogram()
```

Activity: Creating One- and Two-Dimensional Visualizations with a Given Dataset

Steps for Completion:

1. Load the given datasets and investigate them by using the appropriate commands in dataset: xAPI-Edu-Data.csv.
2. Decide which visualizations to use for the given variables: **Topic, gender**, and **VisitedResources**.
3. Create one-dimensional visualizations and explain why you chose that type of visual (one per variable). Provide one point of observation for each visualization.
4. Create two-dimensional boxplots or scatterplots for **VisitedResources** versus **Topic**, **VisitedResources** versus **AnnouncementsView**, and **Discussion** versus **Gender**. What are your observations? Write at least five points.

Outcome:

Three one-dimensional plots and three two-dimensional plots should be created, with the following axes (count versus topic) and observations. (Note that the students may provide different observations, so the instructor should verify the answers.)

The complete code is as follows:

```
df_edu <- read.csv("data/xAPI-Edu-Data.csv")
str(df_edu)

#Functions for Plotting a barchart/Histogram
plotbar <- function(df,mytxt) {
  ggplot(df,aes_string(x=mytxt)) + geom_bar()
}
plothist <- function(df,mytxt) {
  ggplot(df,aes_string(x=mytxt)) + geom_histogram()
}
```

```
#Alternatively one can use a function to plot but students can just
#do it directly at this point.
#1-D Plots
plotbar(df_edu,"Topic")
plotbar(df_edu,"gender")
plotbar(df_edu,"ParentschoolSatisfaction")
plothist(df_edu,"VisitedResources")

#2-D Plots
ggplot(df_edu,aes(x=Topic,y=VisitedResources)) + geom_boxplot()
ggplot(df_edu,aes(x=AnnouncementsView,y=VisitedResources)) + geom_point()
ggplot(df_edu,aes(x=gender,y=Discussion)) + geom_boxplot()
```

Activity: Improving the Default Visualization

Steps for Completion:

1. Use the basic ggplot commands to create two of the plots from *Activity B* (**Topic** and **VisitedResources**).
2. Use the Grammar of Graphics to improve your graphics by layering upon the base graphic. The graph should follow these guidelines:
    1. Histograms should be rebinned.
    2. Change the fill colors of one- and two-dimensional objects. The line colors should be black.
    3. Add a title to the graph.
    4. Apply the appropriate font sizes and colors to the x- and y-axes.

Outcome:

The complete code is as follows:

```
p1 <- ggplot(df_edu,aes(x=Topic))
p2 <- ggplot(df_edu,aes(x=VisitedResources))

p1 +
    geom_bar(color=1,fill=3) +
    ylab("Count")+
    theme(axis.text.y=element_text(size=10),
          axis.text.x=element_text(size = 10),
          axis.title.x=element_text(size=15,color=4),
          axis.title.y=element_text(size=15,color=4))+
    ggtitle("Topics in Education data")

p2 +
```

```
geom_histogram(bins=20,fill="white",color=1)+
ggtitle("Visited Resources for Education data")+
xlab("Visited Resources")+
theme(axis.text.x=element_text(size = 12),
      axis.text.y=element_text(size=12),
      axis.title.x=element_text(size=15,color=4),
      axis.title.y=element_text(size=15,color=4))
```

Chapter 2: Grammar of Graphics and Visual Components

The following are the activity solutions for this chapter.

Activity: Applying Grammar of Graphics to Create a Complex Visualization

Steps for Completion:

1. Use the commands that we just explored to create the scatterplot.
2. For this activity, you will use the gapminder dataset.
3. You can use the help command to explore the options.
4. To change scales, you will have to use one of the preceding label formats.
5. Use labels=scales::unit_format ("K", 1e-3)) for labeling.

Outcome:

The output code is as follows:

```
ggplot(df, aes(x=gdp_per_capita,y=Electricity_consumption_per_capita))+
    geom_point()+
    scale_x_continuous(name="GDP",breaks = seq(0,50000,5000),
                       labels=scales::unit_format("K", 1e-3)) +
    scale_y_continuous(name="Electricity Consumption",
                       breaks = seq(0,20000,2000),
                       labels=scales::unit_format("K", 1e-3))
```

Activity: Using Faceting to Understand Data

Steps for Completion:

1. Use the loan data and plot a histogram (use `fill color=cadetblue4` and `bins=10`).
2. Use `facet_wrap()` to plot the loan data for the different credit grades.
3. Now, you will need to change the default options for `facet_wrap`, in order to produce the following plots.
   Use `?facet_wrap` on the command line to view the options that can be changed.

Outcome:

Refer to the complete code at the following path: `https://goo.gl/RheL2G`. The answers to the questions are given here:

1. `scale=free_y`.
2. A, B, and C have maximum loan amounts below 10,000. (A, B, C, and D is also an acceptable answer.)
3. F and G show uniform distributions.
4. No, none of the distributions are normally distributed.

Activity: Using Color Differentiation in Plots

Steps for Completion:

1. Use the `LoanStats` dataset and make a subset using the following variables:

   ```
   dfn <- df3[,c("home_ownership","loan_amnt","grade")]
   ```

2. Clean the dataset (removing the **NONE** and **NA** cases), using the following code:

   ```
   dfn <- na.omit(dfn)
   dfn <- subset (dfn, !dfn$home_ownership %in% c("NONE"))
   ```

3. Create a boxplot showing the loan amount versus home ownership.
4. Color differentiate by credit grade.

Outcome:

Refer to the following URL for the output: `https://goo.gl/RheL2G`.

The answers to question 5 are as follows:

1. Credit grades F and G are the highest. Credit grades A and B are the lowest.
2. They are higher for a person who has a mortgage.
3. The median value for A is 2,000, and the median value for G is 20,000, so the difference is 180,000.

Activity: Using Themes and Color Differentiation in a Plot

Steps for Completion:

1. Make a scatterplot of female versus male BMIs.
2. Build your plot in layers, to avoid creating three separate plots.
    1. Create the default plot. Store this plot as **p1**.
    2. Points should be differentiated by color. Differentiate the two BMIs by country using color. The size of the points should be 2.
    3. Change the color scheme by using `scale_color_brewer`. The palette used is **Dark2**. Store this plot as **p2**.
    4. Add a plot title: **BMI female vs BMI Male**.
    5. Change more of the theme's aspects to produce plot **p3**. The theme aspects to be changed, and their values, are as follows:
        - Panel Background: `azure`; Color: `black`
        - No grid lines
        - Axis Title Size: 15; Axis Title Color: `cadetblue4`
        - Change x and y titles: **BMI female** and **BMI Male**
        - Legend: Position bottom, Lef justifid, No Legend Title, legend key (fil – `gray97`, color of the line=3)
        - Plot Title Color: `cadetblue4`; Size: 18; Face: `bold.italic`

Outcome:

The output code is as follows:

```
pd1 <- ggplot(df,aes(x=BMI_male,y=BMI_female))
pd2 <- pd1+geom_point()
pd3 <- pd1+geom_point(aes(color=Country),size=2)+
    scale_colour_brewer(palette="Dark2")
pd4 <- pd3+theme(axis.title=element_text(size=15,color="cadetblue4",
                face="bold"),
                plot.title=element_text(color="cadetblue4", size=18,
                face="bold.italic"),
                panel.background =
element_rect(fill="azure",color="black"),
                panel.grid=element_blank(),
                legend.position="bottom",
                legend.justification="left",
                legend.title = element_blank(),
                legend.key = element_rect(color=3,fill="gray97")
)+
    xlab("BMI Male")+
    ylab("BMI female")+
    ggtitle("BMI female vs BMI Male")
```

Chapter 3: Advanced Geoms and Statistics

The following are the activity solutions for this chapter.

Activity: Using Density Plots to Compare Distributions

Steps for Completion:

1. Use the `RestaurantTips` dataset in `Lock5data`.
2. Compare the **TIP** amount for various days. Use `aes=color` for `geom_density` command.
3. Superimpose all of the plots.
4. Use the `scale_x_continuous` command for the *x*-axis tick marks.

Activity: Plot the Monthly Closing Stock Prices and the Mean Values

Steps for Completion:

1. Use the `strftime` command to get the month from each date and make another variable (`Month`), as follows:

   ```
   df_fb$Month <- strftime(df_fb$Date,"%m")
   ```

2. Change the month to a numerical value by using `as.numeric`:

   ```
   df_fb$Month <- as.numeric(df_fb$Month)
   ```

3. Now, use ggplot to make a plot of closing prices versus months.
4. Plot the data using `geom_point (color=red)`.
5. Change the *x* scale to show each month, and label the *x*-axis, such that each month is shown.
6. Title your plot **Monthly closing stock prices: Facebook**.
7. Use `geom_line(stat='summary',fun.y=mean)` to plot the mean.

Outcome:

The complete code is shown as follows:

```
ggplot(df_fb, aes(Month,Close)) + geom_point(color="red",alpha=1/2,position
= position_jitter(h=0.0,w=0.0
))+
    geom_line(stat='summary',fun.y=mean, color="blue",size=1)+
    scale_x_continuous(breaks=seq(0,13,1))+
    ggtitle("Monthly Closing Stock Prices: Facebook")+theme_classic()
```

Activity: Creating a Variable-Encoded Regional Map

Steps for Completion:

1. Merge the `USStates` data with `states_map`.
2. Before merging, change the `states` variable in `USStates` to the same format used in `states_map`.

3. Use the ggplot options `geom_polygon` and `coord_map` to create the map.

4. For aesthetics, run the following code and specify x=long, y=lat, group=group, and `fill=ObamaVote`.

Outcome:

The complete code is shown as follows:

```
USStates$Statelower <- as.character(tolower(USStates$State))
glimpse(USStates)
us_data <- merge(USStates,states_map,by.x="Statelower",by.y="region")
head(us_data)
```

Activity: Studying Correlated Variables

Steps for Completion:

1. Make a subset of the `loan` dataset by using some of the following variables:

```
df3_1 <- df3[,c("funded_amnt","annual_inc","dti","inq_last_6mths",
                "total_acc","total_pymnt_inv")]
```

2. Use `cor` for the preceding `loan` data subset, and then choose two highly correlated variables in the `loan` dataset. Use pairs, as follows:

```
total_rec_prncp and total_pymnt_int
funded_amnt,total_pymnt_inv
```

3. Make a scatterplot for the preceding pairs for grade A, then fit a linear regression model.

4. Determine what are the correlations of the preceding pairs.

Outcome:

Answer to step 4: The correlations are as follows:

1. 93%
2. 85%

Other Books You May Enjoy

If you enjoyed this book, you may be interested in these other books by Packt:

Python Machine Learning - Second Edition

Sebastian Raschka, Vahid Mirjalili

ISBN: 978-1-78712-593-3

- Understand the key frameworks in data science, machine learning, and deep learning
- Harness the power of the latest Python open source libraries in machine learning
- Master machine learning techniques using challenging real-world data
- Master deep neural network implementation using the TensorFlow library
- Ask new questions of your data through machine learning models and neural networks
- Learn the mechanics of classification algorithms to implement the best tool for the job
- Predict continuous target outcomes using regression analysis
- Uncover hidden patterns and structures in data with clustering
- Delve deeper into textual and social media data using sentiment analysis

Mastering Microsoft Power BI
Brett Powell

ISBN: 978-1-78829-723-3

- Build efficient data retrieval and transformation processes with the Power Query M Language
- Design scalable, user-friendly DirectQuery and Import Data Models
- Develop visually rich, immersive, and interactive reports and dashboards
- Maintain version control and stage deployments across development, test, and production environments
- Manage and monitor the Power BI Service and the On-Premises Data Gateway
- Develop a fully On-Premise Solution with the Power BI Report Server
- Scale up a Power BI solution via Power BI Premium capacity and migration to Azure Analysis Services or SQL Server Analysis Services

Leave a review - let other readers know what you think

Please share your thoughts on this book with others by leaving a review on the site that you bought it from. If you purchased the book from Amazon, please leave us an honest review on this book's Amazon page. This is vital so that other potential readers can see and use your unbiased opinion to make purchasing decisions, we can understand what our customers think about our products, and our authors can see your feedback on the title that they have worked with Packt to create. It will only take a few minutes of your time, but is valuable to other potential customers, our authors, and Packt. Thank you!

Index

CPSIA information can be obtained
at www.ICGtesting.com
Printed in the USA
FSHW020535230621
82629FS